NEW LIGHT ON THE STONES OF CALLANISH
written and illustrated by
Gerald Ponting and Margaret Ponting

ISBN 0 9505998 4 0

© **1984 G & M Ponting**
except material otherwise credited and
antiquarian material out of copyright.

Published by G & M Ponting, Callanish, Isle of Lewis

Printed by *essprint ltd. stornoway*

NEW LIGHT ON THE STONES OF CALLANISH
Gerald Ponting and Margaret Ponting

CONTENTS

FOREWORD	3
INTRODUCTION	4
DESCRIPTION OF THE SITE	5
AN OUTLINE HISTORY OF THE SITE	7
A TOUR OF THE SITE	9
THE PREHISTORIC ENVIRONMENT	15
WHO WERE THE CIRCLE BUILDERS?	16
THE BUILDING OF CALLANISH	19
CALLANISH IN THE CONTEXT OF PREHISTORIC SCOTLAND	21
MOVEMENT AND ERECTION OF THE STONES	22
THE SOCIAL CONTEXT OF CALLANISH	25
THE CALLANISH STONES IN LEGEND	27
WHAT TO LOOK FOR AT THE CALLANISH STANDING STONES	28
"CALLANISH", "CLASSERNESS" AND "TURSACHAN"	32
THE ANTIQUARIANS AT CALLANISH	33
A VARIETY OF THEORIES	35
WHAT WERE THE CALLANISH STONES FOR?	40
THE MATHESONS AND THE "RESTORATION" OF CALLANISH	41
MEGALITHIC ASTRONOMY	43
THE MOVEMENTS OF THE SUN	44
THE MOVEMENTS OF THE MOON	45
ASTRONOMICAL THEORIES 1909 — 1977	47
A SUMMARY OF PROFESSOR THOM'S THEORIES	48
"DECODING THE CALLANISH COMPLEX"	51
BIBLIOGRAPHY	53
ACKNOWLEDGEMENTS	55
ABOUT THE AUTHORS	56

Foreword

The Standing Stones of Callanish, on the island of Lewis in the Outer Hebrides, form one of the greatest prehistoric monuments in Europe, Scotland's unique "Stonehenge of the North", dating as far back, perhaps, as 3000 B.C.

Callanish has for long been recognised by antiquarians as a Bronze Age monument of outstanding importance. When the very first *Ancient Monuments Act* was passed in 1882, Callanish was naturally one of the first places to be scheduled for protection. Since then, scholars and laymen alike have endeavoured to "read" Callanish as a document about the past, in an effort to discover something about the culture and mentality of the prehistoric people who built it.

What was it originally intended to be? That is the continuing enigma. A temple? A great funerary complex? An astronomical observatory? Or all three, perhaps? We simply do not know. But under the care of the Secretary of State for Scotland, Callanish is gradually yielding up some of its secrets — or, at least, some additional clues. In the last few years, excavations by the Ancients Monuments division of the Scottish Development Department revealed the existence of a fallen Stone, just outside the original area of ground covered by the 1882 Act, which led to its successful re-erection in its original position — another little help towards our fuller understanding of this remarkable monument.

Gerald and Margaret Ponting have spent ten years studying Callanish as dedicated laymen. Not everyone will agree with some of their ideas on "megalithic astronomy" — a highly controversial subject in academic circles. But this new booklet offers a handy and up-to-date Guide to the monument, which will give visitors a valuable insight into the majesty and mystery of one of the most marvellous achievements of prehistoric Man.

Glasgow
August 1984 **Magnus Magnusson**

INTRODUCTION

In May 1977, after two years' research, we published the first book devoted entirely to "The Standing Stones of Callanish". It proved remarkably successful both as a tourist guide book and as an introduction to the Callanish sites for serious researchers. 13,000 copies have been sold in seven years. But continuing research has added to our knowledge and the book is now out of date in various ways; hence this book.

A number of groups have contributed to this new knowledge since 1977:—

Glasgow University published a definitive plan of the site prepared by students of the Geography Department.

A group of astronomers published the results of their surveying at Callanish.

We have carried out an intensive study of all the old literature about the site.

Pieces of evidence about life in prehistoric times have "turned up" in various parts of Lewis.

An excavation of peat banks near Callanish, begun by us and taken over by the Central Excavation Unit, has produced information on ancient vegetation.

We have made theodolite measurements and astronomical calculations and have presented results to a national conference at Newcastle and to an International Symposium at Oxford University.

Two seasons of "official" excavation at Callanish, and the laboratory follow-up work which will continue for some years, have already revealed much of interest about the site. Initial results were announced at an archaeological conference in Edinburgh in October 1983.

In this book, we attempt to weave all this new material into a more coherent "story" of the Stones than was possible in 1977.

Nevertheless, although partial answers have been found to some of the questions about the site, new questions have arisen. Probably we shall never know the complete Story of Callanish.

DESCRIPTION OF THE SITE

The Standing Stones of Callanish are a major attraction for visitors to the Isle of Lewis. They form one of the most outstanding stone circles in Britain, ranking with Stonehenge, Avebury and the Ring of Brodgar (Orkney).

For the visitor approaching Callanish from Stornoway, on descending from the moor towards the village, the Standing Stones become clearly visible, silhouetted on the skyline ahead. They give the impression of a bristly petrified forest, but are even more impressive as one stands among them.

The Stones are situated on a ridge from which there is a superb view. The waters of East Loch Roag, the mountains of Harris, the hills of Pairc and Uig and the vast open hemisphere of sky formed the backdrop for whatever ceremonies were performed here by prehistoric Man.

The layout of the Stones is unique. In plan, it looks like a Celtic cross, measuring 400 feet from north to south, and 150 feet from east to west. The central circle consists of thirteen stones, ranging from 8 to 12 feet high. The "circle" is slightly flattened, measuring 41 feet from north to south and 38 feet from east to west. Within the circle are the remains of a burial chamber or chambered cairn. When it was "excavated" a hundred and twenty years ago, traces of a cremation were found.

There are five radiating rows of stones. Two of these form an avenue lying a little east of true north. A line of five stones runs south from the circle towards the nearby rocky outcrop of Cnoc an Tursa; another five form a row to the east of the circle; and a row of four runs west from the circle.

This description so far leaves three stones unaccounted for; the largest stone of all (15'9") stands alone within the central circle, and forms part of the rim of the cairn; two more stones (nos. 9 and 35 on the plan) stand just outside the circle to the south east and south west.

This is all that most tourists see of the Callanish Stones, but in actual fact there is much more to see. Within three miles of the "main site" (Callanish I), there are several other stone circles and groups of stones.

SOME OTHER ANCIENT SITES IN LEWIS AND HARRIS

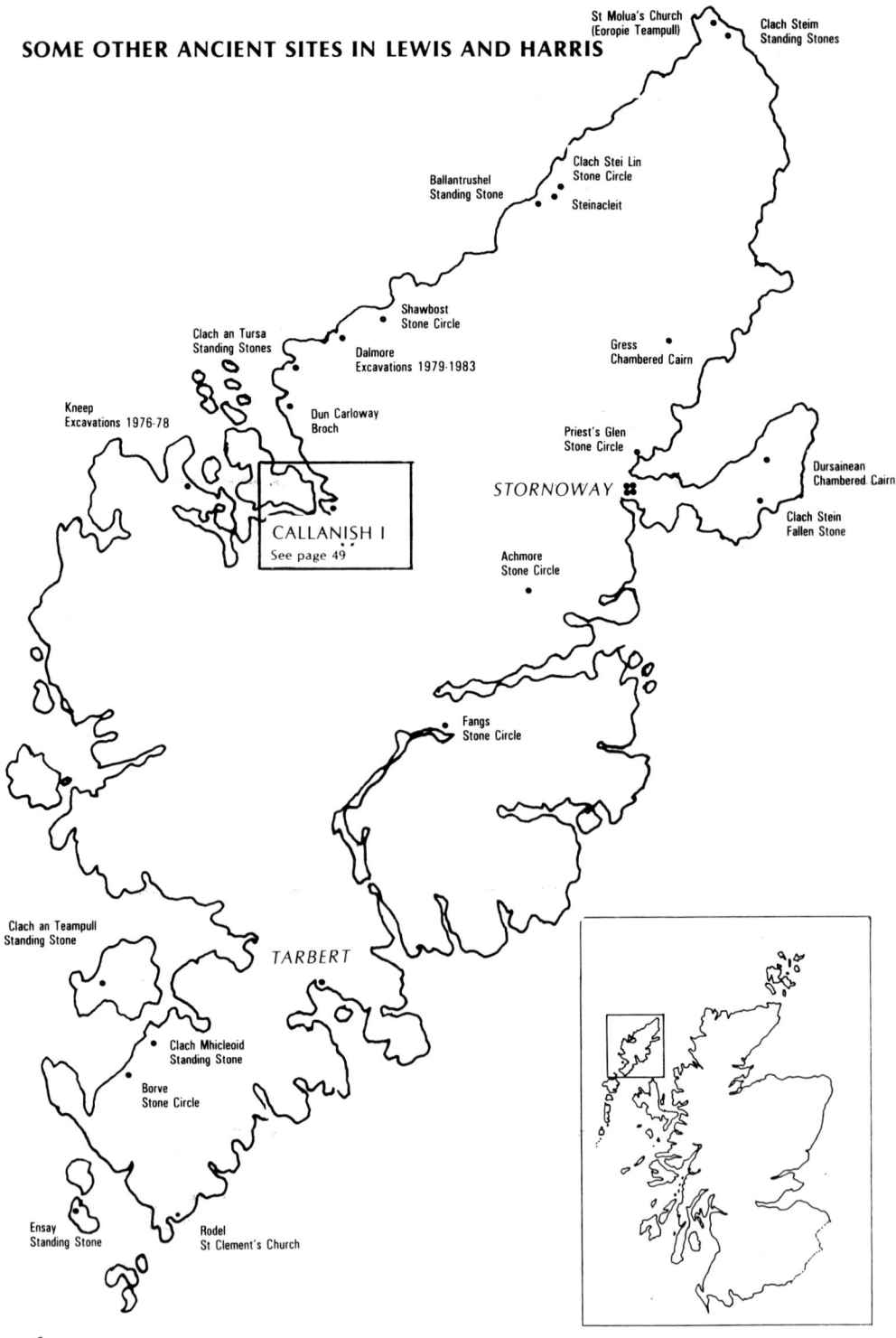

AN OUTLINE HISTORY OF THE SITE

Perhaps as long ago as 3000 B.C. men were ploughing on the ridge where the Callanish Stones now stand. Timber structures of some kind stood there before any stones were erected. We do not know the order in which various stone structures on the site were constructed except that the large central stone must surely have stood in place before the surrounding circle stones.

Perhaps for centuries the circle and the stone rows were used by the descendants of the builders. When people with different traditions moved into the area a tiny burial cairn was fitted between the east side of the circle and the central stone. Even the cairn was built in two phases.

Yet another new culture arrived; they scattered the contents of the burial chamber and ploughed among the stones. Later again, the walling of small stones around the outside of the burial chamber was replaced by the large kerb stones now seen on the north side.

The climate changed between 1000 B.C. and 700 B.C. and peat began to grow on the Callanish ridge. By the seventeenth century A.D. the peat was five feet deep and had completely covered the cairn and some of the smaller stones.

The present Callanish village was settled in about 1790 and a few stones may have been taken for building at that time. The villagers began cutting peat between the stones; by 1854 only the circle and the south row were still semi-engulfed by uncut peat. Once again, after 4000 years, the land around the stones was used to grow crops.

Antiquarians had begun to take an interest in the site around 1700 and a few pre-peat-clearance plans and sketches survive. In 1857 an "excavation" was performed at the direction of Sir James Matheson. The remaining peat was removed from the area of the circle with the result that the burial chamber was revealed. Some restoration of the cairn was carried out shortly thereafter and Stone no. 35 (found lying beneath the peat) was re-erected.

The Callanish site silhouetted against the waters of Loch Ceann Hulavig — which may have been low-lying farmland at the time the site was constructed.

Throughout the latter part of the nineteenth century antiquarian interest increased, with plans, sketches, early photos and descriptions . . . but many of these were based not on first-hand study but on faulty copying from earlier authors!

In 1885 the Callanish Stones were taken into Government protection; since 1939 they have been Government Property.

In the twentieth century Callanish has received more attention from astronomers and geomancers than from archaeologists, but this imbalance has been redressed by the two seasons of major excavation in 1980 and 1981. Stone no. 33A, rediscovered by the authors in 1977, was re-erected in 1982.

We confidently expect that there are more "discoveries" to be made about Callanish — and certainly about prehistoric Lewis generally.

Mr. Neil Macphee of the Ancient Monuments workforce restoring the tip of stone no. 19 in September 1978.

The central megalith of the circle — stone no. 29

A TOUR OF THE SITE

This complements the details on the centre-spread plan and summarises many points described more fully elsewhere in the book.

The Circle and Central Stone

This consists of thirteen stones (nos. 41—53) ranging from 8 to 12 feet high. As Worsaae's sketch of 1846 shows all thirteen stones embedded in five feet depth of peat, there is no doubt that all the Stones stand now as they did in late prehistoric times. Worsaae's evidence is fully confirmed by the Pitt-Rivers notebooks, so those antiquarians recording twelve or fourteen stones were mistaken.

The circle is flattened on the east side and this fits the geometry of Professor Thom's "type A flattened circle".

The large central stone, no. 29, was recorded by all the antiquarian visitors — the only point on which all agree!

The Avenue

There are ten stones on the west side of the avenue, nos. 10—19. Of these, stone no. 19 is the tallest. The tip was restored in 1978, following its discovery by one of the authors (M.P.) in the adjoining field-wall.

On the east side, there are nine stones, nos. 34 and 1—8. Stone no. 34 is not in line with the rest and is best considered with stone no. 9.

The avenue, looking north: on the left, stones nos. 10—19; on the right stones nos. 1—8.

A position at the north end of the avenue, between stones nos. 8 and 19, seems to have been used for astronomical observations, rather than a position within the circle. The midwinter sun set into a hillside and re-flashed in an obvious horizon notch — as seen from the north end, but not as seen from the circle. The avenue lines themselves indicate the southerly extreme moonset into the stones of the circle. Also, the flat face of stone no. 8 indicates a small cliff where the moon sets at its most extreme northerly position.

There are large gaps in the avenue and it is generally assumed that stones have been lost. We attempted to clarify this from our documentary study.

Three plans from the 1850s show the avenue as it is today, and Worsaae's plan enigmatically wanders off the edge of his notebook page. This leaves only Martin's and MacCulloch's plans to give any evidence of the former state of the avenue. There is no independent corroboration of Martin's thirty-nine stones in the avenue, and we believe that the engraver drew this on the basis of a misunderstanding of Martin's text. Some of the stones drawn by MacCulloch are described as "conjectural"; from the remainder, we concluded in 1979 that two stones might have been lost between stones nos. 18 and 19. The 1980 excavation confirmed the loss of one stone in this area (no. 18A). If other stones have been lost from the avenue, this could not be confirmed without more major excavation — which will not occur for many years.

Above, East Row: stones nos. 33A, 33, 32 31 and 30.
Below, West Row: stones nos. 20 — 23.

East Row
The five stones in this row are nos. 30—33 and no. 33A. The last was re-erected in 1982, and the majority of antiquarian sources recorded only four stones. Although MacCulloch drew five stones this was an error and not a record of stone no. 33A — he gave the correct distance from stone no. 23 to stone no. 33 as his overall east-west measurement.

February 1977: the outline revealed by our probing is shown by the circular markers.

May 1980: uncovered by the excavation team. (See also photograph on page 23.)
July 1982: re-erected.

The story of no. 33A begins with a plan drawn in 1857 by Palmer. Most of his measurements were accurate and he included an extra stone nineteen feet beyond stone no. 33. We proved the continued existence of this stone, lying just below the turf, by probing the area systematically with a graduated metal rod. As a result, the area was excavated by "the Ancient Monuments branch of the Scottish Development Department" in 1980 and the stone revealed. Fortunately, its prehistoric socket hole was also found. The site fence was moved to include the new stone, which was re-erected in its true position in July 1982 — five-and-a half years after we had proved its continued existence!

The slightly north-of-east direction of this row has no obvious function unless one accepts star alignments, when there are (inevitably) a number of possibilities depending on the date chosen. It could also have functioned as part of the extrapolation device mentioned on page 52.

West Row
There are four stones in this row (nos. 20—23). As it lies close to due west (four degrees off) it has been assumed to have a connection with the equinox. Somerville suggested observation of the sunset, looking westwards from the circle, while Hawkins suggested watching the sunrise in the opposite direction. Anyone on site on March twenty-first or September twenty-first can check that these events do occur close to this line, but it is not accurate enough for modern archaeo-astronomers. In fact it lies closer to Grid West than to True West!

We believe that the documentary evidence does not suggest the loss of any stones from this row. There is a very slight possibility that stone no. 23 has been re-erected.

South Row

There are five stones in this row (nos. 24—28) though early antiquarians generally showed four, the shortest stone (no. 28) being buried in peat. The last stone in the row is not square in cross section. This is the case in the other four rows and in stone rows elsewhere in Britain; a "blocking stone" defines the end of the row. Perhaps the builders did not need a blocking stone here as the row continued towards the rocky outcrop of Cnoc an Tursa.

This row lies very close to due north-south. If this is accepted as a deliberate intention of the builders, it is a remarkable demonstration of their skill and knowledge. It could have been achieved only by bisecting an angle between a sunrise and sunset, or by bisecting the angle between two extreme positions of a star circling the north pole of the sky.

Stones nos. 9 and 34

Stone no. 34 is frequently taken as part of the east side of the avenue, but it is neither in line with, nor oriented in the same direction as, stones nos. 1 to 8. Stone no. 9 is also an "odd stone out" and many writers have taken it as an indication that there was once an outer circle. However, excavation between stone no. 9 and the west row showed no sign of other "outer circle" stones.

The only theory which proposes an explanation for the position of these two stones is that put forward by Somerville and corroborated by our own survey. An observer standing by the north edge of stone no. 9 and viewing along the flat northwestern face of stone no. 34 would see the full moon rise above the stone when the moon was in its northern extreme position (major standstill).

Interestingly, the setting and re-gleam of the same extreme northern full moon about twenty hours later was indicated by the flat face of stone no. 8 at the other end of the avenue.

Stone no. 35

The first record of this stone, by Sharbau around 1860, described it as "fallen". Earlier visitors had not seen it as it was lying beneath the peat. The Mathesons had it re-erected, certainly before 1867. Within the next eleven years it was broken, reputedly by a drunk waiting for the ferry from Callanish to Great Bernera. Pitt Rivers placed the broken top in position for the purposes of drawing during his 1885 visit and subsequently wrote to Lady Matheson's factor requesting its repair.

However, the stone was still broken around 1900, but was repaired by 1923.

In 1981 the stone was lifted, the concrete removed from its base and a search made for its prehistoric socket hole. Unfortunately this could not be found so the stone was re-erected in its Victorian position.

Its true place in the original layout of the site remains unknown and it must be disregarded in all theories about the former state or function of the site. Notably the idea that it was part of a southern avenue is now untenable.

South Row: stones nos. (9), 28, (35), 27, 26, 25, 24.

Engraving in J. Sinclair's book of 1891, based on a photograph by George Washington Wilson. Stone no. 35, with its top broken off, can be seen in the right foreground.

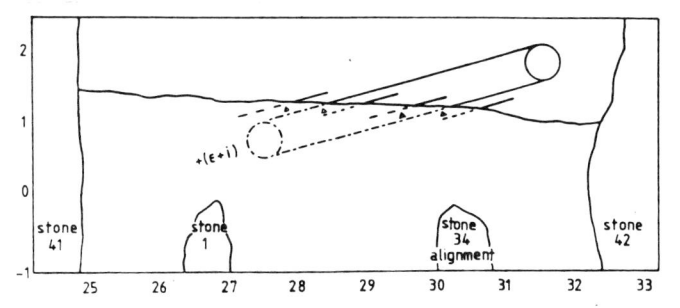

Survey by the authors of the moon alignments first discovered by Somerville. When standing at stone no. 9, stone no. 34 marks the point on the horizon where the moon rose at the northern extreme of the major standstill in prehistoric times. This is still the only theory which provides a possible explanation for the apparently anomalous position of stones nos. 9 and 34.

Stone no. 35, showing the break which occurred around the 1870s and was repaired early this century. It is the only stone at the site known to be in a false position chosen by Victorian restorers.

The Chambered Cairn

29	The large megalith at the centre of the circle.
43, 44	Two megaliths of the east side of the circle which flank the passage.
36, 37,)	Orthostats (uprights) of the chamber, which may have supported
39, 40)	roofing slabs.
38	Shown as a lintel to nos. 36 and 37 by Sharbau. Original position unknown.
40A	This slab was thought to have been a roofing slab until the 1981 excavation, when it was shown to be part of the kerb and was replaced in its present position.
41A	Possible former roofing slab. (The numbers 40A and 41A are used due to a duplication of nos. 40 and 41 by Somerville).
a	A low channel, not very obvious today, thought of as an extension to the passage by some antiquarians, while others described it as a "conduit for blood" from sacrifices! In fact, it was a ditch dug in Victorian times to drain the newly exposed chambers!
b	Entrance passage to the chambers.
c	Larger outer chamber.
d	Smaller inner chamber.
e	The "fill" of the cairn was performed in two stages, the first being a carefully constructed wall following the line of the chamber and the second being a loose fill of rubble between this wall and the kerb.
f	Northern kerb of large slabs placed on edge.
g	Position of former southern kerb, shown in 1980 to be of Victorian origin.
h	Raised pathway from Callanish Farm, constructed in 1860s.

In passage and both chambers, the walling is mostly Victorian reconstruction on a prehistoric lower course. Some parts were taken apart and rebuilt during the 1981 excavation. The curved northern wall of the inner chamber is 1981 reconstruction on a true prehistoric line. The southern wall is Victorian reconstruction — the square corner probably does not represent the prehistoric condition.

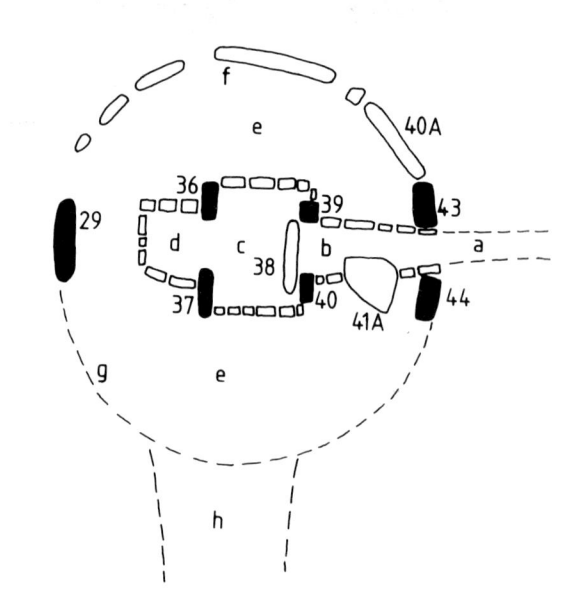

THE PREHISTORIC ENVIRONMENT

The bleak moorlands of Lewis seem an inhospitable place for early man to have chosen as a home. But prehistoric Lewis was very different from the island today. The climate was warmer and drier; the sea level was lower and there was little peat.

The period of stone circle building in the British Isles as a whole (probably 3400 B.C. to 1350 B.C.) coincided with a period of favourable climate — even in Lewis! Overcast, wet and windy weather was quite rare when Callanish was built, an important point for those supporting the astronomical theory of the Stones' use.

It is now known that birch trees grew extensively in at least some parts of the island over 8000 years ago. Possibly these trees were destroyed by the earliest nomadic tribes to reach the island burning areas of forest as a part of their hunting activities. Later the vegetation was a mosaic of willow thickets and copses of hazel and silver birch dotted among the open grassland and heather moor.

This information about past vegetation comes from the study of pollen preserved deep in the peat. Peat forms in cool damp conditions because dead plants do not decay fully when the soil is waterlogged. This partly decayed material generally accumulated at a rate of between half-an-inch and two inches depth of new peat in each hundred years.

In damp low-lying areas peat was forming long before the deterioration of the climate around 1000 B.C. thus providing us with information from even earlier times. Samples taken near the present sea level about half-a-mile from the site reveal a change in vegetation around 1550 B.C. The amount of hazel and birch pollen declines at the level in the peat sample corresponding to this date, while the pollen of grasses and cereals increases. This can be taken as a clear indication of farming tribes clearing the trees and cultivating crops. Samples from elsewhere on the island suggest an earlier date for the introduction of agriculture. (The fact that trees were cleared at a particular date does not prove that this was the earliest clearance in the area. Farming land may have been abandoned for centuries allowing natural vegetation to take over until cultivation was re-started.)

Enlarged about 500 times.

birch

hazel

Even though the land surface of Lewis was more suitable for crops than most of it is today, the favoured dwelling places were probably on the machair — the fertile strips of sandy land behind the Atlantic beaches. Recent excavations at Kneep and at Dalmore have revealed important prehistoric remains.

The Dalmore site is close to the present extreme high tide mark, but must have been on the machair in prehistoric times when the sea level was lower. Similarly, present shallow sea-lochs (such as Loch Ceann Hulavig, close to Callanish) may have been low-lying farmland in prehistoric times.

Some phases at the Dalmore site appear to have been contemporary with some phases at Callanish. If there were other habitations nearer the Standing Stones, it is probable that they were either submerged by the sea or buried by the peat.

WHO WERE THE CIRCLE BUILDERS?

Over 1000 stone circles are known in the British Isles. Many are unspectacular or even ruinous; few have been properly excavated. Excavations which have been carried out have seldom recovered much evidence about how the people lived. It is generally accepted that the circles were communal monuments for families, tribes or tribal groups. If you wanted to find out about the way of life of a modern community, examining individual homes would be more productive than studying churches or community centres.

Quern stone, used to grind grain, found at Dalmore Beach site. 10cm divisions on scale.

This quartz arrowhead, just over 3cm long, is the most finely flaked of all the Dalmore stone tools.

Elaborately decorated pottery sherd of "Beaker" type from the Dalmore Beach site. 1cm divisions on scale.

The recent Callanish excavations did recover finds, such as pottery and arrowheads, and many samples of soil were taken, but it will be some years before the post-excavation research is complete and the full potential of information is realised. We have already mentioned that no local and contemporary habitation sites are known nearer than Dalmore, nine miles away. However, we can use general archaeological knowledge about the circle builders nationally and combine it with knowledge of tools, etc. found on Lewis to provide some picture of the probable way of life of the people who built the circles.

> Archaeologists divide prehistoric times into five Ages. The Palaeolithic or **"Old Stone Age"** need not concern us, as Scotland was still covered by ice for most of the Palaeolithic. The Mesolithic or **"Middle Stone Age"** peoples were hunters who visited or settled some of the Inner Hebrides and may have destroyed Lewis woodlands before 6000 B.C. The peoples of the Neolithic or **"New Stone Age"** were the first farmers and also the first people to settle much of Scotland. These Ages were followed successively by the **Bronze Age** and the **Iron Age**. Each Age has further subdivisions and there is much debate among archaeologists about devising an improved system. The period of stone circle building extended through the Middle and Late Neolithic into the Early Bronze Age, and has been called "Megalithic Times", after the large stones or **megaliths** used in constructing the circles and tombs. Deterioration of the climate occurred in the Middle Bronze Age. By the Iron Age peat was already sufficiently deep to be useful as fuel in the Hebrides.

Our first reasonable assumption is that the builders of Callanish were farmers who grew grain and used saddle querns to make flour. They also kept cattle and sheep, using the meat as food, the skins as clothing and some of the bones to make needles and other tools and ornaments. Deer and other animals were hunted using bows and arrows, and shellfish were gathered from the shore. Fish were caught from the shore or from boats. The people made pottery, often richly decorated, and used it mainly as utensils for food.

Flint, the favoured stone for tools in southern parts of Britain, was almost unobtainable and the occasional pebble of flint found on a beach was much valued for making scrapers and other small tools. In the absence of flint, quartz was used, its abundance compensating for the difficulty of working it. A rock known as baked shale was imported from Skye and flaked to make tools, found solely at Callanish, Dalmore and a few other Lewis sites. At Dalmore, three thumb-nail-sized scraping tools were found, which were very similar in style — one of flint, one of quartz and one of baked shale.

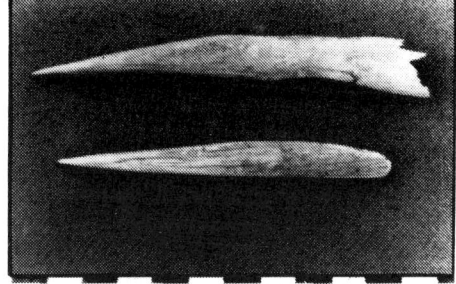

The scraping tools referred to and two sharpened bone tools.   1cm divisions in each case.

We know little about the sort of houses in which the people lived. Certainly timber, stone and turf were all available as building materials. The circle builders were skilled in constructing monuments and in fashioning bone, stone and clay to suit their purposes; no doubt they were equally skilled at building homes from the available materials. Skara Brae on Orkney is a graphic illustration of this — stone which easily splits into flat slabs was used to make "furniture" as though it was wood.

Axes were used to fell trees, for ritual purposes and perhaps for war-like uses. The axe-head was made of stone and the handle of wood. Fine-grained stone made a more easily sharpened axe and, where suitable stone was found, "axe factories" developed. As it is possible to identify the factory of origin of an axe by close examination of the stone, prehistoric trade routes can be traced. It is now well-known that the axe trade ran the length and breadth of the British Isles.

Stone axes have "hit the headlines" in Lewis recently. The first remarkable find, in 1982, was a group of five axes at Balallan, the largest group ever found together in Scotland. Three of the axes were of gneiss and thus probably of local origin; the other two were axe factory products from either Perthshire or Cumbria. The second find, at Shulishader in 1983, was a single axe with its handle well-preserved in the peat — the most nearly complete prehistoric axe ever found in Scotland. The stone is believed to be of Irish origin, but the handle is probably local hawthorn. Both finds are at present in the National Museum of Antiquities in Edinburgh.

The Shulishader axe.
The blade is probably Irish porcellanite, the handle probably local hawthorn.
Photograph by courtesy of the National Museum of Antiquities,
following conservation work on the wooden handle.

The trade in axes seems to answer the question of communications in prehistoric times. We are often asked, "Did the same people build Stonehenge and Callanish?" Putting the question a little differently — were the people who built megalithic sites in Wiltshire and in Lewis, in Cumbria and in Cork, in Shetland and in Brittany able to communicate ideas from one group to another? Travel would have been difficult with swamps, forests and wild beasts on land or the risk of sudden storms while at sea in a flimsy boat. But the axe trade proves that there were those adventurers prepared to take the risks. There is little doubt that ideas would trade no less easily than axes! Sometimes, of course, whole families or tribes may have moved on with livestock and equipment. Archaeological controversy surrounds the question of whether or not the spread of new social customs and pottery styles was accompanied by large-scale movements of peoples.

Another question which has been much debated is whether the circle builders of Britain owed their skills to the Mediterranean civilisations. Until quite recently archaeologists believed that most knowledge originated in the Near East and was carried through Europe to Britain — the circle-builders depended for their "know-how" on early Greece and Egypt. On this theory it was reasonable to think of Callanish as a sort of poor imitation of Stonehenge built by people on the fringe of civilisation. Accurate scientific dating techniques have caused drastic revision of these ideas. Stonehenge I is now known to have been built before the palaces of Mycenean Greece, and Callanish was probably more or less contemporary with Stonehenge III.

The megalithic technology of the British Isles and Brittany owed little to the "diffusion" of knowledge from the Near East.

THE BUILDING OF CALLANISH

Phases of prehistoric activity as revealed by excavation

The first scientific excavation took place in May 1980 and May and June 1981. There were not only various prehistoric phases to distinguish, but also Victorian interference to be investigated. The two seasons of excavation were directed by Patrick Ashmore, an Inspector of Ancient Monuments with the Scottish Development Department who has kindly approved the following summary of his results to date.

A magnetometer survey of the site in 1979 had suggested some areas for excavation. Documentary studies by Patrick Ashmore and by the present authors had indicated places where additional stones might be found. The primary function of the excavation, however, was to obtain information about the cairn area prior to necessary repairs. As the excavation concentrated on the area of the central circle and the cairn within it, little information was uncovered about the radiating rows of stones which are such a distinctive feature at Callanish.

The earliest activity at the site, long before the Stones were erected, seems to have been the digging of a curved ditch. Only part of this was found, due to early agricultural disturbance — the early farmers used a rig system of banks about six feet apart. A piece of pot at this level suggests a date of around 3000 B.C. Ploughing or digging ceased and pasture grew over the tilled soil.

Decades later, holes and trenches were dug into this pasture. It seems likely that posts were erected in these holes as part of a wooden enclosure. The enclosure might have been for stock. However, in view of the next development one might guess that it was some sort of "ritual enclosure".

Next the great megaliths were brought to the site. They were erected in the form of the circle of thirteen stones, with a large central monolith, just as we see them today. It is not known if the north avenue and the south, east and west rows were erected at the same time or later.

The site was not levelled before the erection of the stones. The socket holes dug for the stones seem to have been remarkably shallow. To compensate for this a mound of clay and small stones was built up around the base of each megalith. While the circle was in use, these mounds were clear features and traces of the earlier agricultural rigs must still have been visible.

A new layer of turf developed over the soil disturbed by the "engineering" activity of megalith erection. More holes were dug, at a later date, in this turf, but there is no evidence that timbers stood in these holes.

The next phase of activity probably occurred centuries after the erection of the megaliths. In preparation for the construction of the burial cairn an area within the circle was levelled using puddled clay.

The cairn at Callanish has long fascinated archaeologists. It was apparently designed to fit into the small space between the eastern edge of the circle and the central monolith. Yet, on the grounds that chambered tombs (in general) are older structures than stone circles (in general), some experts have claimed that the cairn was built first.

In the excavations it was shown that much of the cairn material lay over soil disturbed at the time of the erection of the megaliths. Thus, the cairn **must** have been built later than the circle.

In fact, the burial cairn was built in two phases. The second may have been added after an interval of less than a year. The first inner structure was horseshoe shaped, constructed of careful stone walling. It may have been open to the sky, or had a wooden roof. However, the four upright supporting stones (orthostats) seem to have belonged to this phase. This suggests that the roof was composed of large flat "capstones".

The cairn was extended into a circular structure. An outer "kerb" was constructed and the space between the chamber and the kerb was filled with more haphazardly piled stones. When this stage was complete there were certainly capstones over the chamber. Probably there was no great mass of cairn stones piled over them, unlike such tombs as Barpa Langass in North Uist. The completed cairn may have looked rather like a small stepped pyramid.

Later in prehistoric times the cairn was deliberately damaged. Probably, the capstones were thrown off the chambers. The south edge of the cairn was demolished.

Around the same date there was a renewal of ploughing at the site. The soil contained Beaker period pottery, charcoal and five quartz arrowheads. It was not uncommon for burial chambers to be "cleared out" in prehistoric times. The scattered pottery, charcoal and arrowheads may represent the scraped-out contents of the tomb. The possible contents are similar to those found within tombs such as Unival in North Uist. The clearance may have occurred shortly before 1000 B.C.

Strangely, the next event was an embellishment of the damaged cairn. The still-existing northern kerb was built, using large slabs of stone. In all probability these slabs were the former capstones of the tomb. The largest of them (no. 40A) lay haphazardly on the surface till 1981. Two former sockets were found for this stone during the excavations. Evidently it had fallen and been re-erected in prehistoric times. It was placed on edge for the third time by the excavation team.

Adjacent to the circle, to the north east, some kind of structure was built. A scoop in the soil and parts of a wall were found. Victorian activity in the area had obscured the original structure. However, it seems likely that it was a late prehistoric domestic building, standing next to an already disused stone circle and despoiled burial cairn.

Only shortly after this, peat started to form at the site. Over the next three thousand years the peat grew to a depth of five feet, totally engulfing the burial chamber and smaller stones.

Excavation in progress to the northeast of the circle in May 1981.

CALLANISH IN THE CONTEXT OF PREHISTORIC SCOTLAND

Patrick Ashmore's excavation sought not only to discover the phases of activity at the site but also to discover its connections with other sites of similar date. Typically, the pottery found at Callanish gave the first definite evidence. Almost a quarter of the sherds were of distinctively "Hebridean" type.

But the majority of the sherds included categories such as "Grooved Ware", "All-Over Corded" and "Late Northern Beaker" (some of which were also found in the excavations at Dalmore). The significance behind the archaeological jargon is that the types mentioned have a widespread distribution. The various styles also cover quite a wide timescale. (Only the styles were imported; the pottery was probably made locally.)

The existence of the "mainland-style" pottery sherds at Callanish demonstrates an important fact. For 1500 years Callanish was used by people who had a strong and continuing connection with peoples in the areas around the Forth and Clyde valleys. Some of the stone tools found at Callanish were made of baked shale imported from northern Skye.

A plan of the circle at Callanish shows that it is not a true circle. It is flattened slightly on the east side. Professor Thom has shown a means of constructing the shape geometrically and has called it a "type A flattened circle" (see page 49). The ground does not seem to have been levelled before the stones were erected. This led Patrick Ashmore to doubt whether an accurate geometrical method was used. Nevertheless, he pointed out that the suggested geometry of Callanish is identical to that at Temple Wood Stone Circle in Argyll. The only difference is that while at Callanish the geometry fits the outside edges of most of the stones, at Temple Wood it fits the inside edges of the stones.

The actual shapes of some of the stones used at Callanish are very similar to those used in stone circles at Stenness and Brodgar in Orkney and at Machrie Moor in Arran — despite very different geological origins.

The much later structure of the burial chamber does not fit tidily into either the "Hebridean style" or the "Clyde style" of prehistoric tombs. (Three tombs of Clyde type are found elsewhere in the Western Isles.) The nearest parallel to the Callanish tomb is at Nev Hill in Caithness.

Even eighty years ago it was clear to Erskine Beveridge that there were close links in prehistoric times between communities all around the west and north coasts of Scotland. The recent discoveries at Callanish serve to emphasise these connections. We should not think of the Western Isles as an isolated community in prehistoric times.

Nor should we see the islands, as did the nineteenth century antiquarians, merely as stepping stones between Argyll and the Orkneys.

Patrick Ashmore suggested that we should obtain a more accurate picture if we imagined a constant stream of boats to and fro across the Minch. In addition there must have been boats coasting between south west Scotland and the north with Lewis as one port of call — Stone Age forerunners of the West Coast Puffers!

Allowing for this cosmopolitan seafaring element there was a strong local culture. It had its own distinctive style of tombs and its own pottery — and strong cultural connections with the Argyll islands.

MOVEMENT AND ERECTION OF THE STONES

Much has been written about the possible methods by which prehistoric man, with no complex machinery, was able to move and erect large blocks of stone. Most of this material concerns Stonehenge and experiments have been carried out using replicas of the stones there.

The problem at Callanish is, in some ways, a smaller one, as the Stones are of local rock, Lewisian gneiss (unlike the Stonehenge megaliths, some of which were probably transported to Wiltshire from South Wales). It is not certain where the Callanish Stones came from as any one of the many local cliff faces could have provided the slabs. Traditionally, a cliff on Na Dromannan, one mile from the Standing Stones, is regarded as the quarry which was used. Though the stones were not dressed and accurately shaped, like those at Stonehenge, they may have been deliberately prised from the rock face and those of appropriate size and shape chosen for transport.

Logs cut from the then more plentiful trees could have provided a sledge and rollers; ropes could have been made from strips of leather or from heather stems. Each stone could have been pulled to its site of erection by a team of workers using rollers to ease the task — the soil at that time must have been much firmer than the peaty ground today. Avoiding rocky outcrops and choosing the gentlest slope up the rise to the site would have meant a haul of 1¼ miles for each of the forty-nine or more stones.

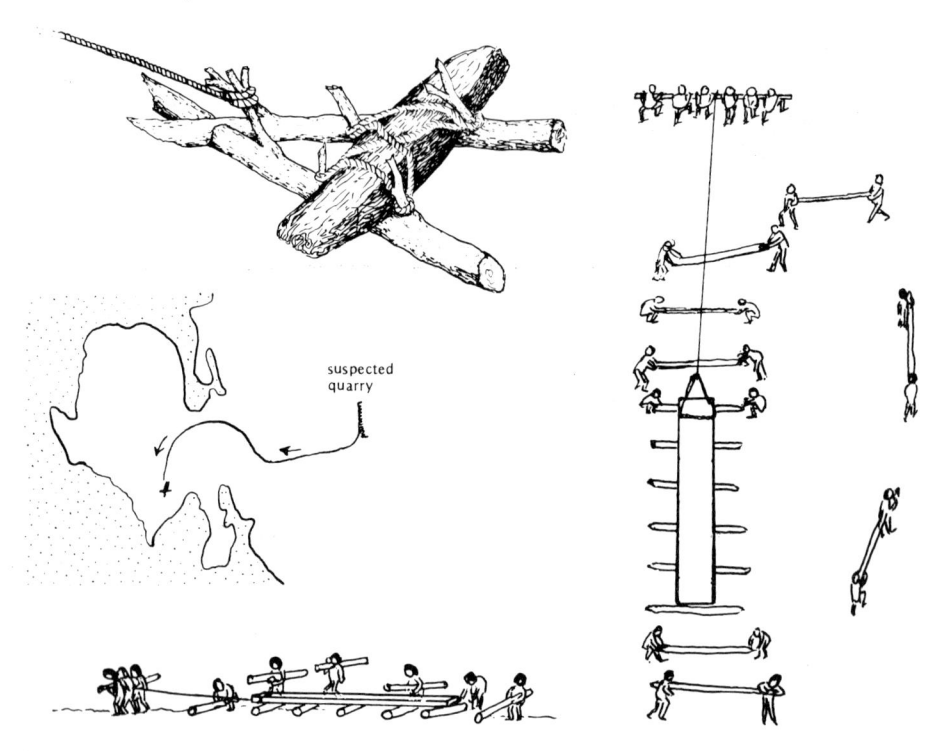

suspected quarry

A socket hole has been dug and partially lined with short stakes. The stone has been brought into position.

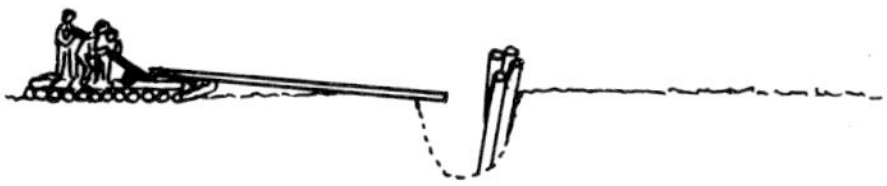

The sledge and rollers have been removed. Workers begin levering at the top of the stone.

As the stone is raised, so the leverage platform is built up with logs. The stakes prevent damage to the edge of the hole.

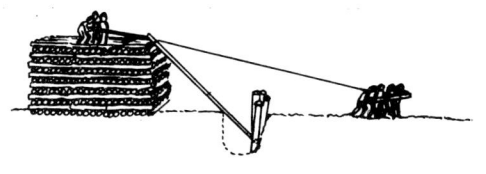

When the leverage platform is high enough, ropes are attached to the top of the stone. Ropes are used to prevent the stone falling sideways as well as to help pull it erect.

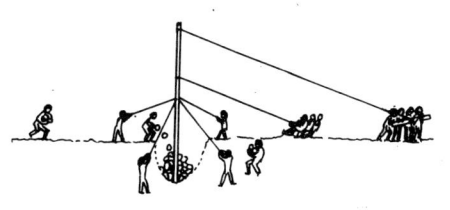

The stone is held in position with ropes while the hole is filled with packing stones and lumps of clay.

The stone is now capable of withstanding Lewis gales for 4000 years, despite the fact that little of it is beneath the surface.

There is no archaeological evidence at Callanish to support this hypothetical description which is based on research at Stonehenge and elsewhere.

During the 1980/81 excavations several socket holes were examined, revealing the packing stones. The large central stone has a large socket hole, shown to be packed with football-sized stones and lumps of clay. While none of the megaliths was excavated down to its base, it was clear from the shapes of incurving lower edges that relatively little of each megalith is buried — probably well under a quarter of the total height in most cases.

The lower tip of stone no. 33A just after refitting into its socket hole. (See also photographs on page 11.) All the stones were held in place by the "packing stones" around the base. 10cm divisions on scale.

The central circle at Callanish in a fresh snow-fall. Diameter of 11m, circle flattened on east, central stone and five radiating rows.

Reconstruction model of the stone circle at Achmore. Diameter of 41m, true circle, no other known features.

THE SOCIAL CONTEXT OF CALLANISH

Why did a group of prehistoric people build such an imposing monument and why did they choose Callanish? How large was the community responsible for raising the Standing Stones?

Any answers to these questions must be speculative, but there are facts which can inform our speculations.

Elsewhere in Scotland there are large numbers of chambered tombs. In Arran it has been shown that there was one tomb for each small farming community and that it was generally situated in a prominent position overlooking the farmland and settlement. These tombs were used not just for burial; they acted as markers of territory and as social and ritual centres. Indeed their social importance was not very different from that of medieval parish churches.

Our studies of previously unrecorded stone circles at Achmore and at Shawbost have emphasised the possibility that in Lewis the many circles may have served the same functions as chambered tombs elsewhere in Scotland.

The weight of the largest stone at Callanish is estimated to be over five tons. Experiments in the Stonehenge area suggest that such a stone could have been moved and erected by as few as twenty-two workers, although this number might need to be doubled to pull it up a slope. If we assume that there were fifty workers, that they were all the able-bodied men of the community and that each worker had about five dependants, a settlement of around two hundred and fifty people **could** have been responsible for the Callanish site. But, if this were the case, the construction of the monument must have been spread over many years. The workers could have worked at the megaliths only in short quiet spells in the agricultural year — perhaps one stone quarried, moved and erected after each harvest was safely stored.

However, this possibility seems unlikely in the context of Lewis with its large number of stone circles. If each smaller circle represents the social centre for a small community, the number of such communities around the head of East Loch Roag was quite high. This area would appear to have been a major centre for the whole island. Translated into episcopalian terms, the small circles were the "parish churches" while Callanish I was the cathedral. Or maybe, as society became more organised, one large centre replaced all the smaller ones. In either case, the workers at Callanish might have been drawn from all parts of the island.

Some other speculations, with less archaeological backing:
1. Each circle in the Callanish area belonged to a different "sect" of some prehistoric religion.
2. The various circles around Callanish all belonged to the same community, but were erected over a period of time, each generation attempting to improve on the work of its ancestors.
3. All the Callanish sites were contemporary and formed an overall "Complex" — a central idea in the astronomical theories.

A composite impression of the Callanish Stones during the process of erection. Note however that the order in which the central circle and the rows of stones were erected is not known.

THE CALLANISH STONES IN LEGEND

Stone circles in all parts of Britain have legends connected with them and numerous authors have collected and collated such traditional stories. Some ideas, such as the stones being uncountable, seem to be very widely distributed. In some cases legends do seem to be a genuine "folk memory" of prehistoric practices.

However, with only two exceptions, all the legends related for Callanish are earliest found in print in Otta Swire's 1966 publication "The Outer Hebrides and their Legends". We suspect that at least some of these "legends" have no local origin, legends from other parts of Britain having been adapted to a Hebridean context. Conversely, we suspect that there are (or were) more genuine legends which will never be vouchsafed to researchers for publication! Despite these doubts, we now summarise all the published Callanish legends which we have found.

- The Stones were brought to Lewis in many ships. They were accompanied by a great Priest-King, lesser priests, and a gang of "black men" who erected the Stones. The workers who died in the process were buried in the circle. When the building was complete, the rest of the black men and some of the priests sailed away, while the great Priest and his remaining assistants set up a cult at the Stones. The priests wore cloaks of coloured feathers, and the Chief Priest always appeared with wrens flying by him.

- Lewis was inhabited by a race of giants, and Callanish was the meeting place for their annual Council. When Christianity first came to Lewis, the giants' Council met to discuss how to destroy this new religion — and St Kieran turned them all to stone!

Midwinter sunset.

27

WHAT TO LOOK FOR AT THE CALLANISH STANDING STONES

The stone numbers shown on this plan are those introduced by Admiral Somerville in 1912. (Stones 36—40 are the slabs of the cairn — see page 14.) The human figures (a—j) indicate points of interest, the letters referring to the notes at the sides of this page.

a The circle consists of thirteen stones, varying from 8 to 12 feet high. They are spaced irregularly around a flattened circle. There is a tradition that "you can never count the Callanish Stones and get the same number twice" — some of the early antiquarians' maps showed only twelve stones in the circle!

a Stone no. 29, the central megalith, is 15'9" high. Till 1857, it appeared about 10 feet high, due to the peat which had grown around the stones. Its weight is estimated at between 5 and 6 tons. Note the large dark crystalline nodule of hornblende high on the east face — these are to be seen on many of the stones at the site.

a Cairn. The central megalith and two of the circle stones form part of the rim around the cairn. The interior consists of two chambers. When excavated in 1857, traces of a cremation were found. The association of this type of chambered cairn with a stone circle is rather unusual. Recent excavations have shown that the cairn was a late addition to the monument, and that it was extensively "restored" in Victorian times. (See detailed plan on page 14).

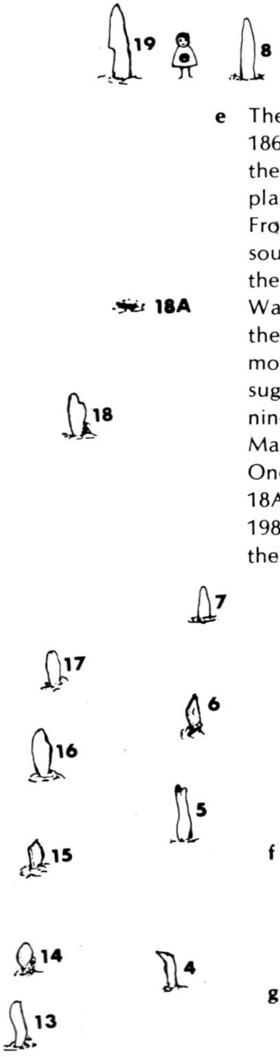

e The tip of stone no. 19 was broken between 1860 and 1885. One of the authors found it in the nearby wall in 1978 and it is now fixed in place again.
From the north end of the avenue, looking south towards the circle, it is easy to see how the idea arose of the avenue as a Processional Way. Cnoc an Tursa forms the horizon beyond the circle, so moonset over the Harris mountains cannot be seen from the avenue as suggested by some researchers. There are nineteen stones in the avenue at present; Martin's plan in 1695 showed thirty-nine stones. One stone definitely known to be missing is no. 18A. The socket for this stone was found in the 1980 excavation. The position is not marked on the site.

f Stone no. 12, now 3'9" high, with a rough flattened top, was 5'2" high when drawn by Sharbau (about 1860). The sharper edges show a recent break.

g The west row is a few degrees off true west, but nevertheless the sunset at spring and autumn

28

b Through the gate at the south of the site is the rocky outcrop of Cnoc an Tursa. From a point on this hillock, it is possible to view along the south row to the central megalith. Somerville was the first to realise that this line was accurately laid out to south/north. The stones of the south row now lean more than in early photographs.

c Stone no. 35 is the smallest erect stone at the site. It was the only stone recorded as "fallen" by Sharbau (about 1860). It has not only been re-erected, but later broken and repaired. As a result of the authors' suggestion that this stone had been re-erected in Victorian times, it was temporarily removed during the 1981 excavation, and found to be set in concrete! Its true position in prehistoric times remains unknown.

d East row. This is a typical alignment, with flat-faced slabs forming an obvious line. Somerville thought it indicated the Pleiades; Hawkins the equinoctial moon; but no definite purpose can be ascribed to it. From this point, two small circles, Callanish II and III, can be seen less than a mile to the east. Several other sites lie further to the south east.

h The last stone in the west row has a much squarer base than the other stones of the row. This is not uncommon in stone alignments throughout Britain. (Note that the end stones of the east row and of the avenue have fairly square bases, but that of the south row does not.) Equinoctial sunrise would be visible along this line through the circle.

i Stone no. 9 stands alone to the south-west of the circle. The best explanation of its position was put forward by Somerville — it forms a lunar alignment with stone no. 34. In 1912, this was the first suggestion that megalithic peoples were interested in the movement of the moon. There is no archaeological support for the idea that stone no. 9 once formed part of an outer circle or a second south row.

j Stone no. 33A was shown on a plan of 1857; lost for over one hundred years; discovered beneath the turf by the authors in 1977; excavated in 1980; and re-erected in its true position on 20th July 1982.

Excursion to the Callanish Stones in about 1905 not by a group of mainland tourists, but members of the Stornoway Gaelic Choir, who had come by gig. Courtesy J. N. Maciver, Garynahine.

- Two Callanish girls loved the same man, and one went to a witch to find a way to remove her rival. The witch gave her a belt, saying that whoever wore it would be snatched away by "her Master". The girl found that she could not do such a thing to her rival, but did not know how to dispose of such a dangerous garment in safety. She thought of putting it round one of the Standing Stones, and when she did so the stone became wrapped in flame, and there were noises as of flapping wings, clanking and howling. She ran home and fainted on the doorstep. The next day, she went with her neighbours and found the stone lying broken and with fire marks where the belt had been. (Local people who know this story today relate it to stone no. 35, which shows a break on it — but this occurred around the 1870s. Also, people recall that lichens were once removed from the stones by burning, which had the effect of "wrapping the stones in flame".)

- About a hundred years ago, certain families in Callanish were known to be "of the Stones", and though the Ministers had expressly forbidden reverent visits to the Stones on the days of the old festivals, they still made these visits in secret, "for it would not do to neglect the Stones". At Midsummer sunrise, "the Shining One" was thought to walk up the avenue, heralded by a cuckoo's call.

- The cuckoo, it is said, also gave its call in time to convene the Druidical May Festival. Nowadays, each cuckoo, on first reaching Lewis in the spring, is supposed to fly to Callanish and give its first call from the Standing Stones.

- During a winter of famine, following a Viking raid on Lewis, a woman met a beautiful white cow coming out of the sea. The cow spoke in Gaelic and told her to bring all her neighbours to the Callanish Stones, where each could take a pail of milk from the cow. Miraculously, the cow was able to give one pail of milk each day to each person, no matter how many came — and this eased the famine. The cow permitted one woman to fill two buckets, as one was for a sick friend, and this gave a witch an idea. She brought two pails for herself, but the cow would not allow the witch to milk her. So the witch came the next day with only one pail, but she tricked the cow by having a bottomless bucket, so that the milk ran to the ground. In this way, she milked the cow dry, and the cow was never again seen at the Stones.

- In the latter part of the nineteenth century, an antiquarian visitor and other members of a house-party at Lews Castle visited the Stones for Midsummer sunrise (but the girls were not allowed to go, as engagements were still formed at the Stones, and men and women together at the circle at such an hour would cause gossip!). An old lady who was "of the Stones" warned them before they set out that there would be a dense mist as "only those to whom it is given may see". This proved true, and the party saw nothing — but heard eerie noises in the mist. It was clear in Stornoway on their departure and their return.

Two remaining stories were not collected by Swire. The first comes from W.C. Mackenzie's "Book of the Lews" (1919) and seems to link the Stones with Druidism. Mackenzie says the story was still current early this century:

- On the first of May (Beltane) all fires on the island were put out. The new fires were lit from one started by an old priest. He lived on a spot, now part of Callanish village, a little way north of the Stones. A tree in a field there was reputed to be the place where he obtained the fire. The fire was distributed by the priest within the stone circle, the people all entering through the "south door" and evil-doers leaving through the "north door".

- At Beltane time a great procession led by white-robed priests chanting songs approached the Callanish Stones. In the procession, the most beautiful woman in the land carried her first-born child for sacrifice. After the child was handed over, the mother (who was not permitted in the "temple") was led to the "place of wailing". This tale was told to Rev. A.C. Maclean in the 1920's in Gaelic by a man of 75. The old man pointed out the wailing place, near the end of the west row, and the "conduit which led the blood away". This conduit or ditch, running eastwards from the burial chamber, has recently been shown to be a Victorian addition to the site! (We suspect that the old man had his tongue firmly in cheek as he told this tale.)

Midsummer morning 1983. A thick mist hid the sun and added a mystery to the Stones — and to the few hopeful visitors. *Photograph by courtesy of R. Harrison.*

"CALLANISH", "CLASSERNESS" AND "TURSACHAN"

The name Callanish was spelt "Callernish" in most 19th century publications, while Martin and his followers had used the spelling "Classerness". Many attempts have been made to interpret the meaning of the word, with varied results. These include:—
- the stones of the judge
- Kali's headland
- keel-shaped ridge headland
- the Bleak headland
- Kjallar's headland (Kjallar was one of the names of Odin)

Those attempts based on Gaelic are doomed to failure. While the names of most hills, streams, bays, etc. in Lewis have a Gaelic origin, the older village names are mostly of Norse derivation. It is noticeable that most of the interpretations include the word headland — "ness" in Norse.

Early in the 1950's, a student from Norway collected the pronunciations of all the village names in Lewis, and attempted to find their meanings in the Old Norse language. He states "Callanish is doubtlessly Old Norse 'Kalladarnes', i.e. the promontory from where one used to call for a ferry-boat to come across a sound". The ferry was probably that connecting Callanish with Linshader. It is worth noting that Callernish in North Uist is situated across the narrow sound from the island of Vallay.

The Gaelic name "tursachan" or "turusachan" is applied to Callanish and to the smaller sites in the area. Its origin is uncertain, but it has been interpreted as the "place of pilgrimage" or the "place of mourning".

Another Gaelic name applied to standing stones is "fir bhreige" — "false men". This seems to take us back to the earliest known mention of Callanish by John Morisone (1680). He quoted the idea that the stones were "men turned to stone by ane inchanter!"

The Form of y Heathen Temple

Martin Martin's plan of the Stones, prepared around 1700. One stone is omitted from the circle and one from each of the south, east and west rows; all the omitted stones must have been visible. We therefore discount this plan as evidence for 19 stones on each side of the avenue. His text is ambiguous, and the plan was probably prepared by "the Hands of some inaccurate Engraver" (Borlase).

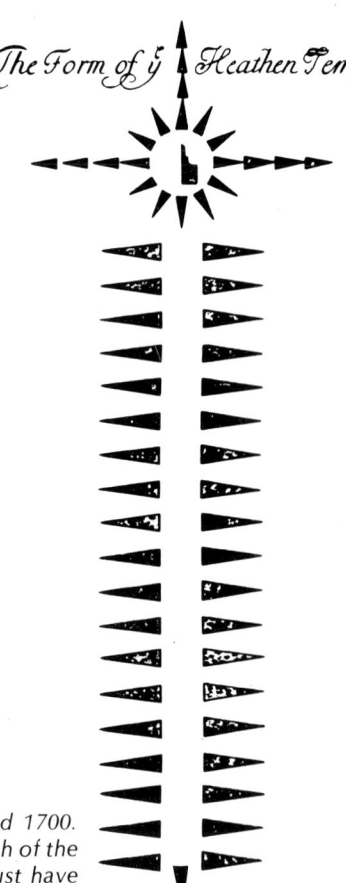

THE ANTIQUARIANS AT CALLANISH

Martin Martin's "Description of the Western Islands of Scotland" (1703) includes the earliest known description and plan of the Callanish Stones. The large number of stones shown on this plan may be due to damage to the site since then, but it is much more likely to have been caused by the engraver's misunderstanding of Martin's ambiguous description.

William Borlase (1754) was the only one to realise some of the errors made by Martin whose plan was widely plagiarised by other authors for over a hundred years.

In 1819, John MacCulloch published the first measured plan of the site, including a number of errors. He showed some stones as "fallen", and this has led to the widespread idea that Callanish is a restored site. We have shown conclusively that MacCulloch's "fallen" stones were actually short erect stones, with only their tops visible above the peat.

> **IS CALLANISH "A RESTORED SITE"?**
> Pitt-Rivers recorded the former level of peat on each stone, still visible when he visited the site, twenty-eight years after the last peat was cleaned. In the case of stone no. 34, a visitor to the site before the peat was cleared in 1857 could have assumed that he saw a fallen stone which had been around four feet tall. MacCulloch had recorded this stone as "fallen" in 1819, for this reason. The same sort of argument can be applied to **all** of MacCulloch's fallen stones. All the statements that Callanish is a "restored" site are based on the idea that MacCulloch's fallen stones must have been re-erected last century. But there were no fallen stones, other than no. 35.
> Callanish is a remarkably intact site.

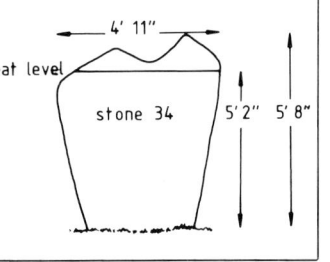

Jacob Worsaae *(pronounced "vor-so")*, a prominent Danish archaeologist, visited Callanish in 1846. His field notebooks, now in Copenhagen, contain the earliest drawings of Callanish — made when five feet of peat still enveloped much of the site. His drawing of the circle, together with Sir Henry James' post-peat-clearance drawing, make it clear that all the circle stones remained erect throughout the period of peat growth.

At around the time of Matheson's 1857 "excavation" *(see page 41)* John Palmer made a good plan of the site and Sharbau drew the stones individually. This makes it clear that stone no. 35 was the only stone found lying beneath the peat, and thus the only one which was "restored" last century.

From the 1840's onwards, and particularly after the publicity connected with the excavation, there was a steady flow of visiting antiquarians. A number of them made plans and drawings, of various degrees of accuracy. A reference to the Standing Stones of Callanish became obligatory in any book on prehistoric Scotland, and was included by many authors who had not visited the site. The second edition of James Logan's "The Scottish Gael", published six years after the excavation, still included a wildly inaccurate plan based on a combination of Martin's and MacCulloch's plans.

In 1882 the Ancient Monuments Protection Act was passed. Three years later General Pitt-Rivers, the first Inspector of Ancient Monuments, visited Callanish. Later the same year, Lady Matheson gave permission for the site to be taken into Government guardianship.

Pitt-Rivers' records of his visit, now scattered in Edinburgh, London and Salisbury, provide invaluable information concerning the site. His measurements of each stone and of the former peat level mark on each stone have enabled us to draw our conclusions about MacCulloch's "fallen" stones and have also helped in tracing the individual histories of some stones.

Pitt-Rivers' work marked the watershed between antiquarianism and true archaeology, though the only full archaeological description of the site appeared in the "Outer Hebrides Inventory" of the Royal Commission on Ancient and Historical Monuments of Scotland (published in 1928 based on surveys in 1914 and 1923).

Facsimile of a letter from Lady Mary Jane Matheson to Gen. Augustus Pitt Rivers dated October 15th 1885. The key section reads,"I shall only be too glad to have "the Callernish Stones" and the "Doune" put under the Ancient Monts. Acts and quite believe that it is the only way to preserve them. . . . ."

Courtesy of Salisbury & South Wilts Museum.

34

A VARIETY OF THEORIES

From 1680 till the present day, there have been many published speculations on the original function of the Callanish Stones.

Jacquetta Hawkes wrote in 1967 that "Every age has the Stonehenge it deserves — or desires" and the same could be said of the theories proposed since 1680 to explain Callanish. In the eighteenth century Druids were popular; in the twentieth century they have been replaced by scientifically-inclined astronomer-priests.

We now give each of the main theories, and some variations, in chronological order of publication. Each is expressed either in the author's own words or as a summary of the author's opinions with our comments in italics. Analysis of modern astronomical theories comes in a later section.

John Morisone c.1680: *(Callanish not mentioned by name)*
" . . . In severall places (in Lewis) there are great stones standing up straight in ranks . . . It is left by traditione that these were a sort of men converted into stones by ane Inchanter, others affirme that they wer sett up in place for devotione."

Martin Martin 1703
"I enquired of the Inhabitants what Tradition they had from their Ancestors concerning these Stones; and they told me it was a Place appointed for Worship in the time of Heathenism, and that the Chief Druid or Priest stood near the big Stone in the center, from whence he address'd himself to the People that surrounded him."

William Stukeley c. 1720
Callanish was a Druid temple of a type known as a "Dracontium" or serpent temple. *Stukeley never visited Callanish and thought the avenue "serpentine". The circle-and-serpent symbol represented the divine creator.*

John Toland 1726
The twelve *(sic)* circle stones represent the Zodiac; the four "side-arms" represent the four winds; and the nineteen stones on each side of the avenue *(sic)* represent the 19-year cycle. Thus the temple was dedicated principally to the sun and subordinately to the seasons and elements (the seas and the winds).

T. Carte 1747
Callanish was the "winged temple" of Apollo mentioned by Eratosthenes. The nearby circle was probably dedicated to the moon. The people of the Hebrides were the Hyperboreans mentioned by Herodotus. Every nineteen years gifts were taken from Callanish to the holy Greek isle of Delos.

William Borlase 1754
The fifty-two *(sic)* stones in the avenue and circle and the twelve *(sic)* stones in the east, west and south rows represented the numbers of weeks and months in the year.

James Headrick 1808
Callanish was a "rude astronomical observatory". " . . . the priests could mark out the rising of the sun, moon, and stars; the seasons of the year; even of the hours or divisions of the day."

*The central circle at Callanish drawn in 1846 by Jacob Worsaae — the earliest known picture of the site. Comparison with the modern photo taken from Worsaae's viewpoint shows the height of the peat on the circle stones. Worsaae stood on a surface five feet above the present ground level when he made his sketch — the photograph was taken from a step-ladder.
From Worsaae's original field notebook with the permission of the Nationalmuseet, Copenhagen.*

R. Huddlestone 1814
The Druids had both religious and judicial circles. The nearby circle was the temple, the main Callanish site was a judicial circle, the supreme court of the Hebridean monarch.

John Pinkerton 1814
"The noble circle ... (was) ... an ancient gothic court, in which great affairs were decided; the avenue, &c. being mere pieces of rude magificence."

John MacCulloch 1824
In satirical mood, MacCulloch demolished the Druid ideas of earlier authors, by quoting two alternative astronomical interpretations of Callanish: either, the central stone represents the sun and the stones of the circle the planets (if the Druids followed Copernicus) or, the north-south line of the site represents the meridian and the east-west line the ecliptic (if the Druids followed Ptolemy). MacCulloch's own opinion was that all stone circles were of Norse origin and were used as temples, courts, theatres and funeral monuments. From its size and style, Callanish was probably a temple to Thor.

Henry Callender 1854
Looking along the south row to the central stone enables accurate observation of the Pole Star. *But there was no Pole Star in prehistoric times!*

John Palmer 1857
On an otherwise useful plan, Palmer refers to the central monolith as "the Callanish Phallus" — implying that the Stones were a fertility temple.

Thomas MacLaughlan 1863
The ground plan represents a Celtic cross. The site is Christian and its construction was either a penance for a very grievous offence or "merely the offspring of Christian zeal".

John Stuart 1866
Callanish is similar to a large burial chamber like New Grange (Ireland) without the covering mound, the avenue representing the passage and the circle representing the chamber.

Engraving of Callanish from the east by James Kerr, included in Henry Callender's paper of 1854. Peat cutting has progressed along the east row, but the central circle is unaffected. The rock in the bottom right hand corner is stone no. 33A after it fell but before it was covered by new peat growth.

J. Fergusson 1872
He accepted Stuart's idea. As New Grange is of the Christian era *(actually Neolithic)*, Callanish must be also. Like chambered tombs, it was probably built by a great king during his lifetime for use as a tomb and memorial when he died.

W. Anderson-Smith 1874
Callanish was a Norse construction, combining the pagan style of temple with a ground-plan in the shape of a Christian cross. It was built probably in the eleventh century A.D. The other circles round about are Norse "Things" or open-air annual parliaments.

T. Wise 1877
There were four avenues at Callanish, each made into a passage by palisades. These four approaches were used by different classes — north for the military, south for the peasantry, east for merchants and west for priests. Worship occurred at sunrise and sunset, with the priests standing by the central stone and "honest supplicants" bearing gifts of food and flowers. Prayers were offered with sacred hymns and chants. The symbol of the deity hung on the central stone.

A.L. Lewis 1900
Callanish was a "sun and star" circle, with the south row aligned on the Pole Star and stone no. 34 indicating midsummer sunrise.

A.C. Maclean 1926
Callanish was the "resting-place of the illustrious dead" in the Bronze Age. As a secondary use it became a great pagan sanctuary for religious festivals.

Norman Morrison 1936
"Abaris was the Arch Druid of the Callernish Temple (which was dedicated to Apollo), the great druidical Cathedral of Scotland." *Abaris, in classical writings, was a Hyperborean who visited Athens receiving a wonderful arrow from Apollo.*

Tom Lethbridge 1973
Martian survey parties were dropped at various points around the Earth to look for minerals. They built Callanish and other monuments as landing marks for the flying saucers which were due to pick them up. Wild dancing around the ring charged the stones with "bio-electrical potential" which saucers could detect.

John Michell 1974
Callanish was the centre from which human sacrifices were embarked for the Flannan Isles, where "the Little People" accepted the tribute sent to them. This also explains the Flannan Lighthouse mystery. The group of keepers who disappeared in 1900 had been sent out from the village adjoining Callanish . . . and this new "tribute" was accepted despite the lapse of many centuries!

Donald Cyr 1976
As well as forming indications for sunrise and sunset on particular days, the stones also probably indicate the position of false suns ("sun-dogs") *(see photo on inside back cover)*. Although these are rare meteorological occurrences today, this theory supposes that they were common in megalithic times, due to a hypothetical layer of ice crystals in the upper atmosphere left over from the previous Ice Age.

Lynne Wood 1981
Rituals relating to birth, fertility and death were enacted in the circle. This awakened the White Goddess and revitalised the people and the environment of the island. The Callanish circles, together with other sacred sites throughout Britain, formed a network of communication, involving the vital forces of life, for universal enlightenment.

An attempt by "earth energies" enthusiasts, who concentrate on the mystical aspects of ancient sites, to link Callanish into a "Chackra system" involving sites throughout Britain

CALLANISH - Brow
TWELVE APOSTLES - Throat
CASTLERIGG - Heart
ARBOR LOW - Navel
ROLLRIGHT - Sex
AVEBURY - Root
BOSCOWEN-UN - Foot
GLASTONBURY TOR - Knee

Commentary on the theories

John Aubrey originated the theory that British stone circles were Druid temples and the idea first appeared in print in 1695. It may be more than a coincidence that this was about the time that Martin Martin was compiling his account of Callanish!

The main exponent of the idea in the first half of the eighteenth century was William Stukeley. Ably assisted by Toland and Huddlestone, he convinced most of the academic world.

The 1936 entry above is a remarkably late version of the Druidical theory and in style is very similar to books written over a hundred years earlier.

The theory is effectively destroyed now, as the Druid cult came into being around a thousand years after the last stone circle was built. However, it is possible that, in some cases, the Druids were the inheritors of rituals connected with stone circles which were already ancient in their days.

Druids normally used oak groves as their sanctuaries and there is no real evidence that the cult ever reached the Hebrides. (This does not prevent Callanish being referred to, to this day, as "the Druidical Stones"). Stuart Piggott's book on the "The Druids" deals with all these points very fully.

If it seems surprising how many authors thought of the Stones as a Norse or Christian structure, it should perhaps be pointed out that the word "prehistoric" was coined only in 1851. The periods of human history were not clearly distinguished until well into the last century.

While modern astronomical ideas are dealt with later in this book, it is worth noting that several authors already quoted connect the Stones with the sun, moon or stars. Headrick's idea that the Stones were an "astronomical observatory" predates Professor Thom's theories by almost one hundred and fifty years.

The ideas of Michell, Lethbridge and Wood are typical of many writings on the fringes of archaeology today which involve all kinds of unknown forces. The best-known example is the theory of ley lines, but there is little published material linking Callanish with the British "ley network".

One of the most apt pieces of speculation about the functions of the Stones comes not from an antiquarian journal but from a popular Victorian novel, "A Princess of Thule". The author brings his chief characters to the Stones — Lavender, a young man-about-town on a visit to Lewis, and Sheila, the "princess of Borva" (Great Bernera).

William Black 1873

"... Lavender had paid but little attention to the "false men" of Callernish when first he saw them, but now he approached the long lines of big stones up on this lonely plateau with a new interest. For Sheila had talked to him about them many a time in Borva, and had asked his opinion about their origin and their age. Was the central circle of stones an altar, with the other series marking the approaches to it? Or was it the grave of some great chieftain, with the remaining stones indicating the graves of his relations and friends? Or was it the commemoration of some battle in olden times, or the record of astronomical or geometrical discoveries, or a temple once devoted to serpent worship, or what? *Lavender, who knew absolutely nothing at all about the matter, was probably as well qualified as anybody else to answer those questions* ..."(Our italics.)

WHAT WERE THE CALLANISH STONES FOR?

We can never know the aims of people who lived thousands of years ago. Even if we were able to use a time machine to watch the activities once performed in stone circles, we should not be able to enter the minds of megalithic people.

Aubrey Burl, the author of several excellent books about British stone circles, believes that ceremonies connected with death dominated the rituals in the circles. In some parts of Britain it seems likely that circles were trading centres on the known axe trade routes.

One thing which we should remember is that cultures which live in balance with their environment see fewer distinctions between the various aspects of their lives than do (so-called) civilised societies. To megalithic people, as to present-day jungle tribesmen, science, religion, medicine, agriculture, and everyday life probably formed a single complex of thought and ritual. If we ask, "Were the Callanish Stones a temple, a calendar, a community centre, a crematorium, or a status symbol for the tribe?" the answer may be, "Yes, all of these at the same time, without distinction."

A stone circle probably had a multi-purpose use. The building of the circle was a communal effort and the completed result formed the focus for all the activities important to the community — for instance, worship of the sun, the moon, or some other deity; dancing, trading, initiation ceremonies, marriages, funeral rites and so on. The festivals of the agricultural year including planting and harvest were probably celebrated in the circle; as were the extremes of the solar year, midsummer and midwinter, and the equinoxes half-way between these extremes. Callanish, like other British stone circles, may have been a "combined temple and community centre" in one imposing site. This of course still leaves open a fascinating question: if a plain ring was usually satisfactory, why did Callanish develop into a more complex shape?

Engraving of Callanish published 1867 by Sir Henry James, Director of the Ordnance Survey. The marks left on the stones when the peat was cleared ten years earlier were still very clear.

THE MATHESONS AND THE "RESTORATION" OF CALLANISH

Sir James Matheson made his fortune in the Far East, largely through the opium trade from India to China. He was able to retire in his forties, buy the Isle of Lewis with the proceeds, and devote the rest of his life to "good works". He spent vast amounts on "improving" the island. His home was Lews Castle in Stornoway, now a technical college.

At the suggestion of Henry Callender and the Society of Antiquaries of Scotland, Sir James had the peat removed from around the stones of the circle at Callanish in October 1857. (The villagers' peat cutting activities had already cleared the peat from the avenue.) No detailed record was made of this "excavation", but a letter from Sir James to the Society described the discovery of the chambered cairn in the centre of the circle:—

"The average depth of the moss (= peat), from the surface to a rough causewayed basement in which the circle stones were imbedded, was 5 feet, and the workmen had not proceeded far with their operations, when, in front of the large centre stone and extending to the eastern wing, they came upon an erection which proved, as the work proceeded, to be the walls of a chambered building, consisting of three compartments, . . . The larger chamber was found to have two stones on each side, forming jambs for the entrance to the smaller chamber; and in close proximity to these, there was found a separate stone, 4 feet long by 12 inches, which fitted, and was supposed to be a lintel to the jambs referred to. These stones were rough and unhewn . . . I enclose some minute fragments of what we suppose to be bones found in the chamber, and a specimen of a black unctuous substance, in which these fragments were contained."

The Society submitted the samples to Professor Anderson, who definitely considered the fragments to be burnt human bones, and the unctuous substance to be "peaty and animal matter combined, but after so great a lapse of time, he could not speak with certainty as to this". A local tale, still current, is that a great deal of "charcoal" was uncovered at the excavation, and used for drawing on the Stones by local children.

The letter continued — "It is remarkable that the sides of the small chamber are quite undisturbed — not a stone even of the uppermost tier removed from its place . . .". The 1980/81 excavations have shown this statement to be quite untrue. Most of the walling seen today is of Victorian origin, or careful reconstruction after the 1981 excavation. However, the lower courses of stones are genuinely prehistoric. (See illustration on page 42.)

In fact, the Mathesons or their Factor ordered a quite extensive "reconstruction" of the cairn. Stone no. 35 was re-erected in a position chosen at the time. As some of the black houses of Callanish were adjacent to the Stones and cultivation was going on close by them, some crofts were re-arranged to clear the area around the Stones.

Lady Matheson had a path made up from Callanish Farm (then an inn, and the nearest place which could be reached by horse and carriage). The slightly-raised path entered through the south gate. It is seen most easily today just to the south of the stone wall, where it curves down the hill towards the Farm. The path made it easy for Lews Castle house-parties to visit the site without risk of soiling the ladies' long dresses!

The burial chamber at the centre of the cairn, drawn by Sharbau not long after it was first uncovered in 1857. The "lintel" at the back now lies within the chamber (stone no. 38) — it is probable that it was balanced in the position shown purely for the purposes of this drawing. The original is a very faint pencil sketch in the National Monuments Record and is reproduced with their permission (Crown copyright). This version has been "inked in" on a photographic enlargement of the original.

Below, chambered cairn after the 1981 restoration, photographed from the same angle.

MEGALITHIC ASTRONOMY

Following earlier vague suggestions relating the site to the sun and moon, a number of twentieth century authors have attributed precise astronomical functions to the Stones. A little basic astronomical background is necessary before it is possible even to summarise these theories.

Many people are satisfied with vague statements like "the sun rises in the east and sets in the west", but this is too simplified. The movement of the position of sunrise along the eastern horizon, and of sunset around the western horizon, would have been much more significant to prehistoric peoples than it is to modern city dwellers. Also, the degree of movement is much more marked in a northern latitude like Callanish.

Many people know that one of the Stonehenge trilithons forms an archway for viewing the sunrise over the Hele (or Heel) Stone on midsummer's day. But few people realise that two stones, or a line of stones, are sufficient to indicate the position of sunrise or sunset on a particular day. Such alignments of stones are found throughout Britain, and their study is known as **megalithic astronomy**, a branch of the young science of **archaeo-astronomy** (study of the relationships between ancient sites and the movements of sun, moon and stars).

If megalithic Man did deliberately set out astronomical alignments (and some archaeologists still doubt this), he did so in a practical manner. Observations of the movements of the sun or moon could have been made and then recorded with the help of wooden stakes, which were later replaced by stones.

To record a horizon position permanently, the "indication" may be an alignment of two or more stones in a row, a viewing line from one site to another, or simply sighting along the flat face of a single stone. In any of these cases, the indication may "point" to some prominent horizon feature — a mountain peak or a "notch" between two hills, where the rising or setting sun or moon would have been seen on the appropriate date. If the sun or moon set behind a hill then reappeared in a notch ("re-flashed" or "re-gleamed"), then the indication was especially accurate. *(Continued on page 46.)*

THE MOVEMENTS OF THE SUN

The sun's position on the eastern horizon at sunrise and on the western horizon at sunset varies throughout the year. This variation is greater the further one travels from the equator — this explains why there are more hours of daylight in northern Scotland in summer than in southern England. The diagram shows the six most significant solar events, with relevant data for Callanish.

On the diagram, the central point represents the position of the "observer" standing at a stone alignment. The radiating lines represent the directions in which sunrise and sunset can be seen at different dates. The direction is quoted as an **azimuth — which is measured in degrees clockwise from True North (for example: E = 90°, S = 180°, W = 270°).** The dates of the spring and autumn equinoxes and of the summer and winter solstices can vary by a day or two from those given and should be checked with an almanac. The times and azimuths quoted are approximate — the main variation is caused by the height of the horizon behind which the sun is rising or setting.

The arcs on the left and right of the diagram represent the annual swings of sunset and sunrise position respectively. It takes a full year for the sunrise position to swing from one extreme to the other and back again — the sunset position behaves as a 'mirror image" of the sunrise position.

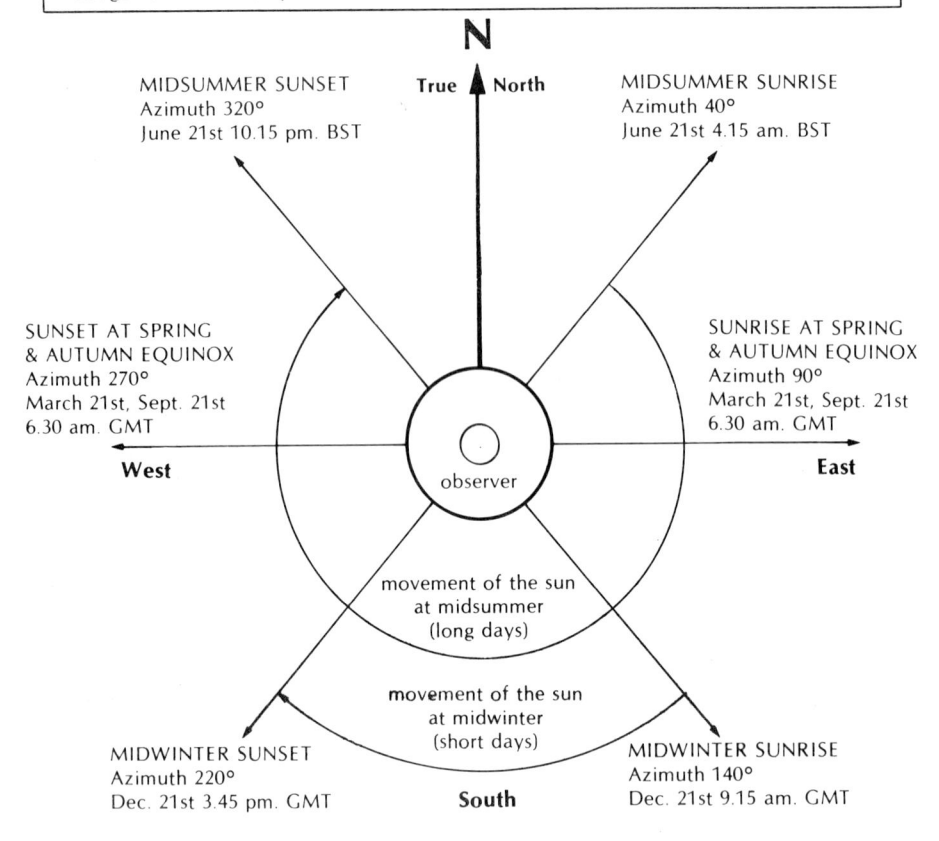

N

True ↑ North

MIDSUMMER SUNSET
Azimuth 320°
June 21st 10.15 pm. BST

MIDSUMMER SUNRISE
Azimuth 40°
June 21st 4.15 am. BST

SUNSET AT SPRING
& AUTUMN EQUINOX
Azimuth 270°
March 21st, Sept. 21st
6.30 am. GMT

West

observer

SUNRISE AT SPRING
& AUTUMN EQUINOX
Azimuth 90°
March 21st, Sept. 21st
6.30 am. GMT

East

movement of the sun
at midsummer
(long days)

movement of the sun
at midwinter
(short days)

MIDWINTER SUNSET
Azimuth 220°
Dec. 21st 3.45 pm. GMT

South

MIDWINTER SUNRISE
Azimuth 140°
Dec. 21st 9.15 am. GMT

Times and azimuths are approximate and assume a horizon level with the observer.
The dates of the equinoxes and solstices (midsummer and midwinter) can vary by a day or two.

THE MOVEMENTS OF THE MOON

The swings of moonrise and moonset across parts of the eastern and western horizon are similar to those of the sun, but occur monthly, not annually, with about thirteen swings a year. But, due to the tilt of the moon's orbit, the length of the swings varies over the months. **A complete cycle, from "major standstill" to "minor standstill" and back again, is completed in 18.61 years.** (The moon never "stands still" — the term refers to the repetition of a similar pattern of movements over several consecutive months.)

At minor standstill in 1978, the swings of moonrise and moonset around the horizon were at a minimum. The moon rose at "A" and set at "B"; a fortnight later, moonrise occurred at "C" and moonset at "D".

Over the following 9.3 years, the monthly swings increase towards a maximum. At the major standstill in 1987, moonrise and moonset will be at "W" and "X"; a fortnight later at "Y" and "Z".

(The rise and set of the full moon at midwinter has been used by some researchers as equivalent to the northern extremes and the rise and set of the full moon at midsummer as equivalent to the southern extremes.)

The actual observation of the moon at these various extremes is complicated by the phases of the moon. Moonrise and moonset are most spectacular when the moon is full; but at new moon, it is impossible to observe the rise or set for several days.

Further complications arise from the possibility of unfavourable weather conditions when the moon is, briefly, at its extreme position; from our present uncertainty whether it was the upper or lower part of the moon's disc which was recorded on the horizon and from a minor "wobble" in the moon's orbit.

Modern archaeo-astronomers must take into consideration all of these matters most of which would have caused real difficulties for the original observers in megalithic times.

If one finds positions W, X, Y and Z marked by megalithic "pointers", we can only marvel at the patience required by prehistoric man to achieve these records of the lunar extremes — a kind of "Book of Records" in stone.

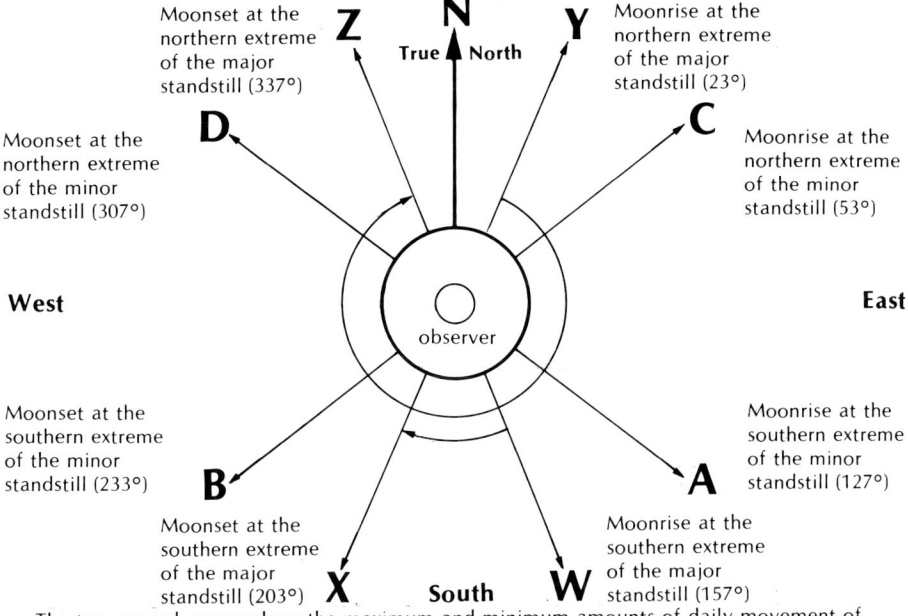

Moonset at the northern extreme of the major standstill (337°) — Z

True North — N

Moonrise at the northern extreme of the major standstill (23°) — Y

Moonset at the northern extreme of the minor standstill (307°) — D

Moonrise at the northern extreme of the minor standstill (53°) — C

West

observer

East

Moonset at the southern extreme of the minor standstill (233°) — B

Moonrise at the southern extreme of the minor standstill (127°) — A

Moonset at the southern extreme of the major standstill (203°) — X

South

Moonrise at the southern extreme of the major standstill (157°) — W

The two curved arrows show the maximum and minimum amounts of daily movement of the moon, in relation to the horizon, at the major standstill which occurs every 18.61 years.

> To verify a suspected alignment today, complex calculations are necessary. From the azimuth of the alignment, the latitude (58° 12'N for Callanish), the height of the horizon, the degree of bending of light rays by the atmosphere, etc., it is possible to calculate an indicated position in the sky. Making allowances for slight changes during the last 4,000 years in the relationship of the sun, moon and earth, one can discover if this "indicated position" matches a significant position of the sun or moon in megalithic times. Meticulous work with theodolite, camera and electronic calculator is required to carry out such studies.
>
> To produce valid scientific proof that "megalithic Man" did deliberately set up astronomical alignments, such calculations must be performed for many alignments and all the results studied statistically. However, the destruction of many sites in the past has reduced the amount of data available to the statisticians. There may no longer be enough sites left intact for a valid analysis. This underlines the importance of preserving apparently insignificant sites today, and of making horizon surveys before viewing lines are blocked by new building. It also increases the importance of non-statistical evidence in megalithic astronomy.
>
> Nevertheless, the possibility of a statistical "answer" to the astronomical theory puts it in a different category from the other theories — it **is** capable of scientific verification.

The most obvious practical use for a "megalithic solar observatory" would have been to establish and maintain an accurate calendar, to which the operations of the agricultural year could be linked. Such calendars are known to have been used by primitive tribes in recent times. Contact between communities for trade or other purposes (see pages 17, 18 and 21) might well have required agreements as to the dates of meetings, e.g. the third full moon after midsummer.

A megalithic lunar observatory could have been used to predict "eclipse seasons" — the times when eclipses of the sun and moon occur. Eclipses are events which produce terror in primitive tribes. An astronomer-priest who could give prior warning of an eclipse, and also promise that all would return to normal if the tribe paid tribute at the observatory-temple, would have a high status.

There are four directions most likely to have been marked at a megalithic lunar observatory — the rise and set positions at both the northern and southern extremes of the major standstills (Y, Z, W and X on the diagram). It would have taken several generations to establish these positions, but traces of wooden stake-holes at Stonehenge provide strong evidence that it was done.

The corresponding four positions of the minor standstill (C, D, A and B) are less obvious, but are believed to be marked at some sites.

Stonehenge was built at a particularly significant latitude for the sun; in a similar way, Callanish was built near a unique latitude for the moon. For a few days in each 18.61 years, the moon rises so close to due south that its path across the sky (from rise at "W" to set at "X" in diagram on page 46) is less than 2° above the horizon. In other words, the path of the full moon just skims above the horizon. *(See diagram on page 50.)* (In the north of Shetland, the moon never rises at all at the southern extreme of the major standstill.)

All of this presumes a much greater intellect for prehistoric Man than previously supposed. But his brain size was equal to ours — there is no real reason to regard him as less capable of abstract mathematical thought than we are.

ASTRONOMICAL THEORIES 1909 — 1977

The first scientifically-based astronomical theory was proposed by Sir Norman Lockyer in 1909. He never visited Callanish, but found two "star-rise" lines using published information.

The azimuth at which a star rises changes considerably over the centuries, and some archaeo-astronomers have used alignments with stars to date the erection of the stones. But this is a process of doubtful validity; and in any case, star rise is very difficult to observe. Star alignments seem much less likely to be present in megalithic monuments than sun and moon lines.

Rear Admiral Boyle T. Somerville, a naval hydrographer, made surveys at Callanish in 1909. His plan of the site, published three years later, remained definitive (despite several inaccuracies) till the survey by Glasgow University Geography Department appeared in 1978. He introduced the numbering system for individual stones which we have used in this book, with some adaptation due to Somerville's accidental duplication of some numbers. He identified two "star-lines", one "sun-line" and, significantly, one lunar alignment.

Stone nos. 9 and 34 indicate the horizon position of the rising moon at the northern extreme of the major standstill. We have confirmed this with our own surveys, but there is no prominent feature on the horizon. Somerville was the first to suggest that prehistoric man — anywhere — was concerned with accurate observation of the moon.

Gerald Hawkins, a Professor of Astronomy working in the USA, published a list of twelve astronomically significant alignments at Callanish in 1965. A follow-up to his famous work "Stonehenge Decoded", the Callanish results were obtained by a computer study of Somerville's inaccurate plan. Indeed, five of the lines involved Stone no. 35, and there is no evidence that any stone stood at that point in prehistoric times.

Hawkins' pioneering work is largely superseded today, especially as all his alignments are too short to be acceptable to modern archaeo-astronomers. Hawkins also published an accurate survey of Callanish, which compares well with the "Glasgow Survey"; unfortunately it is almost unobtainable in Britain.

Long before Hawkins began his studies, the other great pioneer of megalithic astronomy had been researching the subject for many years.

Alexander Thom, a former Professor of Engineering, carried out a long-term and meticulously detailed study of the megalithic sites of Britain and Brittany. Even archaeologists who reject his remarkable theories respect the enormous amount of detailed research which lies behind them. Thom visited many hundreds of sites, carried out his own surveys, and subjected his results to statistical analysis. In the 1970s and 1980s, much of this work was done in partnership with his son, Dr A.S. Thom.

Professor Thom was first inspired to begin his studies on a visit to Callanish in 1933, when he wondered how prehistoric man could have laid out the south row as an accurate north-south line, without a Pole Star as a reference point.

Thom's work at Callanish has been largely overtaken by subsequent discoveries, but it would be difficult to imagine modern megalithic studies without the tremendous stimulus given by Thom's work. Our own involvement with archaeology began with a fascination with Thom's "Megalithic Sites in Britain" and the encouragement which he gave us in correspondence.

A SUMMARY OF PROFESSOR THOM'S THEORIES
as published in his three books and many scientific papers.

1. Megalithic Man was capable of complex astronomical and geometrical thought.
2. The stone circles and other groupings of stones are set out, not only to indicate astronomical events, but also to satisfy definite geometrical criteria and in a limited number of geometrical shapes. For instance, many of the "circles" are flattened on one side, in an attempt to give the ratio of circumference to radius (v) a value of three rather than three-and-one-seventh.
3. The axes and perimeters of these circles, and many other measurements, were often laid out in exact multiples of 2.72 feet (0.829 metre). Thom calls this the Megalithic Yard (MY).
4. The Megalithic Yard was standard throughout Britain (implying a centralised production and distribution of "Megalithic Yardsticks"?).
5. At some sites, the megalithic astronomers refined their methods of lunar observations by the use of distant mountain peaks and "notches", sometimes in conjunction with complex arrays of stones. In this way, they could measure the movements of the moon very accurately, even to the extent of discovering the slight wobble (of nine minutes of arc) in the moon's orbit. This would have given them the ability to predict eclipses with improved reliability.
6. Indications of sunrise and sunset points intermediate between those for the solstices and equinoxes would give "intermediate calendar dates", thus dividing the year into sixteen or even thirty-two "epochs" (Thom's term for a megalithic "month").

Thom's ideas about Callanish, reviewed in the light of new information.

★ The central circle is a "Type A Flattened Circle".
(Although Thom did his work using Somerville's plan, this statement is not invalidated by the Glasgow University plan, with a slight change in orientation).

★ The lines of the east and west rows, and the central line of the avenue meet at "point C", in the geometry of the flattened circle.
(The Glasgow University plan makes it clear that these lines do not cross at a single point. At Temple Wood stone circle in Argyll, stone pegs were found at significant points in the "Thom geometry", but nothing similar was found in the excavations at Callanish).

★ An ellipse of small stones to the north-east of the main circle may have been involved in midsummer sunrise observation.
(Excavation made it clear that the "ellipse" was a complex feature containing both prehistoric and Victorian elements).

★ The two stone rows which make up the avenue are eleven MY apart, but not absolutely parallel. They could have aligned with **both** the rise of the star Capella to the north (as suggested by Somerville) **and** with moonset into Clisham at the southern extreme of the major standstill.

★ The east row indicates the rise of the star Altair in 1800 B.C., the same date that Capella would have aligned with the avenue.

(Star-rise is generally discounted by archaeo-astronomers today. The avenue could not have been used for accurate moonset observation, as Clisham is hidden by Cnoc an Tursa. However, we have shown that this moonset was a spectacular event when viewed down the avenue *(see diagram on page 50)*.

★ Eleven inter-site lines between the various sites in the Callanish area may have astronomical significance. (See next section).

Another group whose work was stimulated by Thom's studies visited Callanish in 1975 and published their results in 1977. John Cooke, Roger Few, Guy Morgan and Clive Ruggles, all astronomy graduates, surveyed sight-lines at and between eight of the sites in the Callanish area. Their intention was to test a new approach to archaeo-astronomy. Dr. Ruggles has continued this work professionally for some years, attempting to gather a body of data as large as Thom's, but in a form which Ruggles considers more suitable for statistical analysis.

The team found all the astronomical indications suggested by Somerville, Thom and Hawkins, except one at Callanish V, to be invalid. We consider that this result was inevitable, given their methods.

The results of our own archaeo-astronomical research at fourteen sites in the Callanish area have been published in two papers under the general title of "Decoding the Callanish Complex . . ."

"Type A Flattened Circle" geometry applied to the Glasgow University plan.   Courtesy of G. R. Curtis.

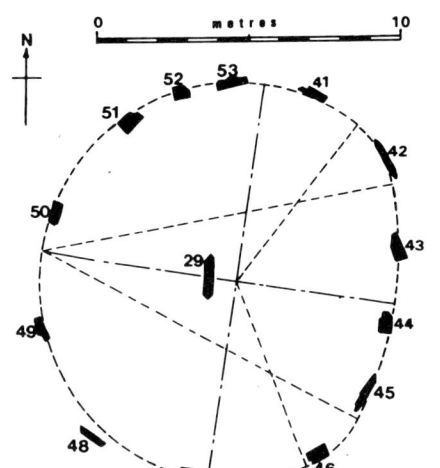

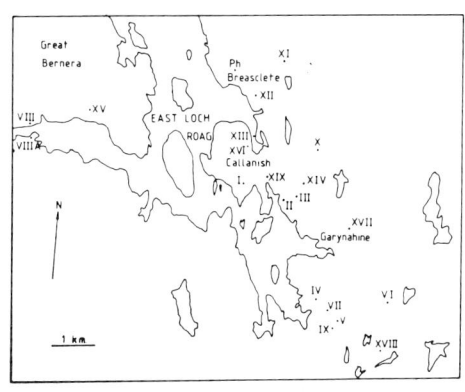

Map showing distribution of megalithic sites around the head of East Loch Roag.

ASTRONOMICAL ALIGNMENTS AND THE CALLANISH "MINOR SITES"

Three small stone circles in the Callanish area were known to early antiquarian visitors. Professor Thom numbered the Callanish area sites from Callanish I to Callanish VII; the Glasgow University team continued to Callanish XII; and we have brought the system up to Callanish XIX. It is beyond the scope of this book to include descriptions of all these sites, not all of which have been confirmed as definitely prehistoric.

However, with the requirement that astronomical sight-lines should be longer than those provided by stones within an individual site, several archaeo-astronomers have investigated lines from one site to another. Thom recognised eleven inter-site lines with possible astronomical significance.

There are three hundred and forty-two possible lines between nineteen sites. We have examined each of these possible lines on the ground, and found that two hundred and twenty were intervisible, and therefore worth investigating for astronomical indications.

In a companion volume to this book, "The Stones Around Callanish", the minor sites are described and illustrated.

The forerunner of this book, "The Standing Stones of Callanish", included pictures and comments on sites II, III, IV, V, VI, VIII and XII.

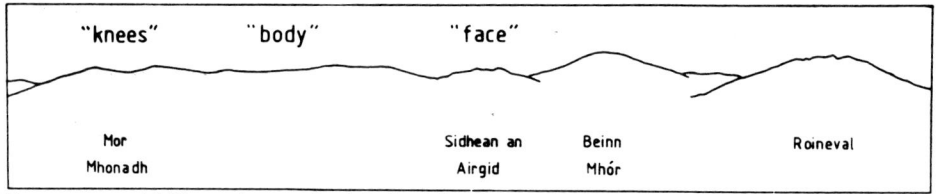

Two ranges of hills to the south of Callanish: above, the "Sleeping Beauty" range in Pairc in southeast Lewis; below, the Clisham range in North Harris.

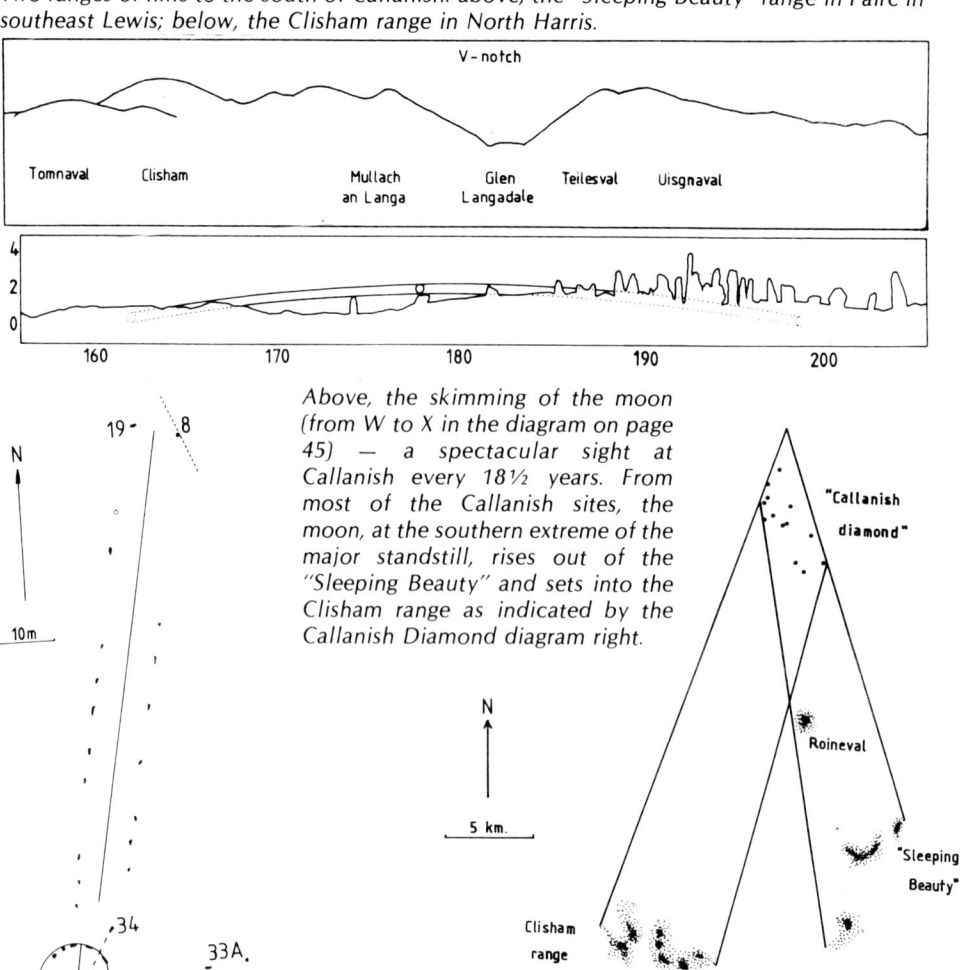

Above, the skimming of the moon (from W to X in the diagram on page 45) — a spectacular sight at Callanish every 18½ years. From most of the Callanish sites, the moon, at the southern extreme of the major standstill, rises out of the "Sleeping Beauty" and sets into the Clisham range as indicated by the Callanish Diamond diagram right.

Plan showing astronomical alignments suggested or confirmed by the authors. The solid lines show the central line of the avenue and the long axis of the flattened circle — these are parallel and point to the set of the moon at the southern extreme of major standstill. This may have been a ritual occasion with the full moon making a spectacular sight as it set within the stones of the circle. The dashed line shows the alignment of stones nos. 9 and 34; the dotted line shows the direction indicated by the flat face of stone no. 8.

50

"DECODING THE CALLANISH COMPLEX"

We have used this title for lectures on our own astronomical studies given at two conferences. The Proceedings of the 1980 Newcastle Conference have been published as "Astronomy and Society in Britain 4000 — 1500 B.C.", while those of the 1981 International Archaeoastronomy Symposium at Oxford have appeared as "Archaeoastronomy in the Old World". Anyone with a deeper interest in the astronomy of the Callanish sites should read our papers and those of other speakers in these two volumes. Here we must summarise and inevitably simplify.

Several of the minor sites incorporate alignments which record the horizon positions of moonrise and moonset at the standstills — A, B, C, D, W, X, Y and Z on the diagram on page 45. In some cases, the moon "re-gleams" in a mountain notch. These sites were the megalithic observatories. Our initial results suggest that the megalithic astronomers were particularly interested in the southern extreme of the major standstill — that skimming of the southern horizon by the moon which is so spectacular at the latitude of Callanish.

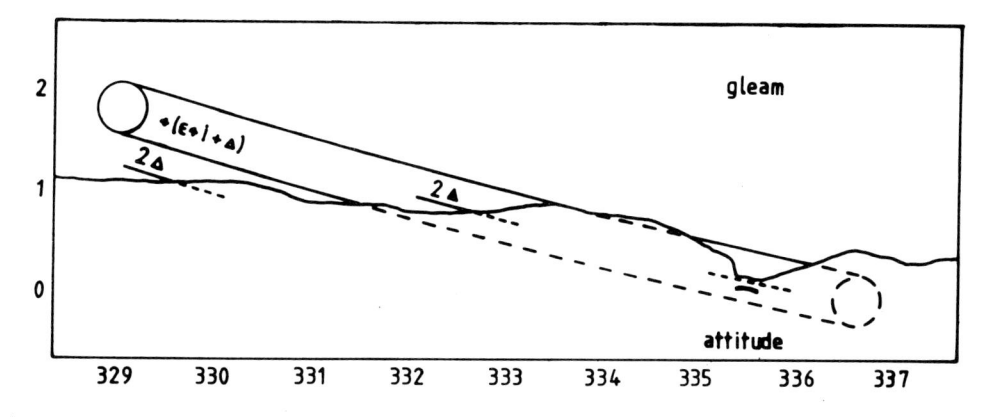

Above, moonset at the northern extreme of the major standstill. The small cliff-face where the moon "re-gleams" after setting is indicated by looking along the flat face of stone no. 8. Below, the clearest of the moon alignments at the minor sites. From site XVII (Druim na h-Aon Chloich) the moon "re-gleams" in the deep v-notch immediately above site IV (Ceann Hulavig). **In all horizon diagrams** *the numbers along the bottom are degrees of azimuth while those on the left are degrees of apparent altitude above a level horizon.*

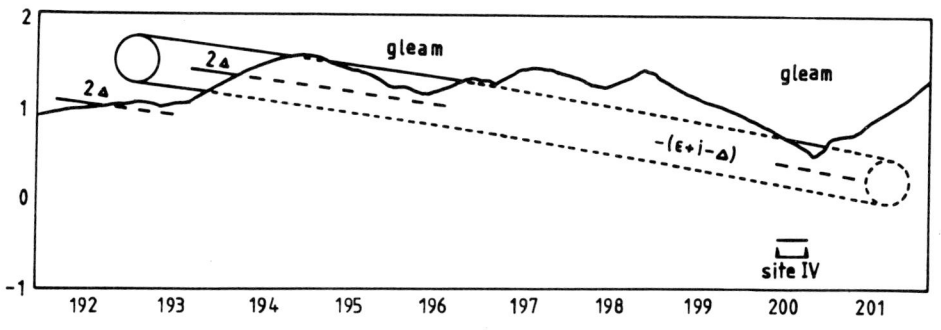

This skimming of the horizon fits in very well with the idea that Diodorus (a Greek historian) was describing Lewis when he wrote about the Hyperboreans in 55 B.C.; though "Hyperborea" could be anywhere well north of Greece.

"... there is also on the island ... a notable temple which is ... spherical in shape ... the moon, as viewed from this island, appears to be but a little distance from the earth ...... the god visits the island every nineteen years ...... the god ... dances continuously the night through from the vernal equinox until the rising of the Pleiades ..."

The small "circles" around Callanish are all either ellipses or flattened circles. In each case, the long axis of the ring is directed to a solar or lunar extreme — rather as many Christian churches are orientated with their axes lying approximately east-west.

At the main site, the south row defines a north-south line, (extended by an outlier, site XVI, about eight hundred and seventy-five yards north of the central stone); stones nos. 9 and 34 indicate the northern extreme moonrise; while the flat north east face of stone no. 8 indicates the setting and re-gleam of the same moon. The long lines of the avenue guide the eye of observers standing at the north end of the site to the circle. At the southern extreme, the moon, after skimmimg low over the hills, would appear to set into the stones of the circle. From the same position, the midwinter sun set into a mountain and re-flashed in a notch; if this was formerly indicated by stones or by stakes, it provided the means of checking an annual calendar.

The observatory sites required a means of "extrapolating" their results, using a geometry based on ropes and pegs. We have shown that the stones of the avenue could have been used as a basis for this. If this were done, eclipse seasons could have been predicted.

A suggestion in our 1980 conference paper offered an explanation for the concentration of sites in the Callanish area. All the sites lie in an area which we have called "the Callanish Diamond". From this region the hills of Pairc in SE Lewis and the hills of North Harris are particularly suitable for observation of the rising and setting moon at its southern extreme. Was the area chosen for its relationship to these two groups of hills?

The Pairc hills form the profile of a sleeping woman, which is well-known to the inhabitants of Callanish. The hills do not have this appearance from other villages. Sometimes called the Sleeping Beauty, her Gaelic name is less flattering — Cailleach na Mòinteach (the old woman of the moors). Since we pointed out the relationship of the southern extreme moonrise with this range of hills, the "Earth Energies" enthusiasts have linked this with the worship of the White Goddess and the pagan "universal earth mother" — which was **not** part of our theories!

At sites in Great Bernera, and at Clach an Tursa in Carloway, we found similar lunar indications, using entirely different ranges of hills. We believe that there is already good evidence that the movements of the moon were an important consideration in the layout of both individual sites and of the whole Callanish Complex. Hopefully, in due course, there will be sufficient technical data available to convince even the statisticians.

BIBLIOGRAPHY

Anderson-Smith, W. 1874 **Lewsiana**. Paisley.
Ashmore, P. 1980 **Callanish 1980 Interim Report.** Edinburgh. Scottish Development Department, Ancient Monuments Division.
Ashmore, P. 1983 **Callanish — Recent Excavations.** Lecture at conference: Neolithic and Bronze Age Settlement in the Western Isles. Edinburgh.
Atkinson, R.J.C. 1959 **Stonehenge and Avebury.** London.
Borlase, W. 1754 **The Antiquities of the County of Cornwall.**
Callender, H. 1854 Notice of the Stone Circle at Callernish, in the Island of Lewis, **Proc. Soc. Antiq. Scot., 2**(1854—7), 380—4.
Camden, W. 1695 **Britannia.** London.
Carte, T. 1747 **The History of England.** London.
Cooke, J.A., Few, R.W., Morgan, J.G. and Ruggles, C.L.N.
1977 Indicated declinations at the Callanish megalithic sites. **J. Hist. Ast., 8,** 113—133.
Cowie, T. 1979 **Callanish (Leobag) 1979 Interim Report.** Falkirk: Central Excavation Unit.
Curtis, G.R. 1979 Some Geometry associated with the Standing Stones of Callanish. **Hebridean Naturalist, 3,** 29—40.
Cyr, D. 1976 Expedition to Scotland, **Stonehenge Viewpoint** (Santa Barbara, CA), Vol. 8 no. 4, 1—10.
Fergusson, J. 1872 **Rude Stone Monuments.** London.
Hawkins, G.S. 1965 **Stonehenge Decoded.** New York.
Hawkins, G.S. 1965 Callanish, a Scottish Stonehenge. **Science, 147,** 127—130.
Hawkins, G.S. 1971 Photogrammetric survey of Stonehenge and Callanish. **National Geographic Society Research Reports — 1965 projects,** 101—108. Washington D.C.
Headrick, J. 1808 Editorial notes *in* G. Barry, **History of the Orkney Isles.** London.
Henshall, A.S. 1972 **The Chambered Tombs of Scotland, Vol. 2.** Edinburgh.
Huddlestone, R. 1814 Editorial notes *in* Toland, J., **The History of the Druids.** Montrose.
Innes, C. 1858 Notice of the Stone Circle of Callernish in the Lewis, and of a chamber under the Circle recently excavated, **Proc. Soc. Antiq.Scot., 3** (1857—60), 110—2.
James, H. 1867 **Stonehenge and Turusachan in the Island of Lewis.** Southampton.
Lethbridge, T.C. 1973 **The Legend of the Sons of God.** London.
Lewis, A.L. 1900 The Stone Circles of Scotland, **J. Anthrop. Inst., 30,** 56—72.
Lockyer, N., 1909 **Stonehenge and other British Stone Monuments Astronomically Considered.** *(Second Edition.)* London.
Logan, J. 1831 **The Scottish Gael.** Inverness.
MacCulloch, J. 1819 **A Description of the Western Islands of Scotland.** London.
MacCulloch, J. 1824 **The Highlands and Western Islands of Scotland.** London.
Mackenzie, W.C. 1919 **The Book of the Lews.** Paisley.
Maclaughlan, T. 1864 Notice of Monoliths on the Island of Mull, **Proc. Soc. Antiq. Scot., 5** (1862—4), 50ff.
Maclean, A.C. 1926 Callernish, or Ross-shire in the Bronze Age, **Scottish Notes and Queries, 3rd series, Vol. IV,** 49—51, 69—71, 92—95.
Martin, M. 1703 **A Description of the Western Islands of Scotland.** London.
Michell, J. 1974 **The Flying Saucer Vision.** London.
Morisone, J. c.1680 Description of the Lewis by John Morisone, Indweller There, *in* Macfarlane, W, **Geographical Collections,** Edinburgh (1907).
Morrison, N. 1936 **Hebridean Lore and Romance.** Inverness.
Oldfather, C.H. (translator)
1935 **Library of History, Book II, by Diodorus of Sicily.** Cambridge (Mass).
Oftedal, M. 1952 The Village Names of Lewis in the Outer Hebrides, **Norsk Tidskrift for Sprogvidenskap,** Bind XVII.
Palmer, J.L. 1857 Unpublished plan. **National Monuments Records,** RCD/13/18.
Piggott, S. 1968 **The Druids.** London.
Pinkerton, J. 1814 **An Enquiry into the History of Scotland.** Edinburgh.
Pitt-Rivers, A. 1885 Unpublished plan. **National Monuments Record,** RCD/13/4.
Pitt-Rivers, A. 1885 onwards Letters and personal papers. **Salisbury and South Wilts Museum,** AM10.
Pitt-Rivers, A. and Tomkin
1885 Unpublished notebooks. **Public Record Office,** WORK39/15 — 6.

53

R.C.A.H.M.S.	1928	**Inventories of Ancient Monuments, Vol. 9: Outer Hebrides, Skye and the Small Isles.** Edinburgh.
Sharbau,	c.1860	Manuscript plans and drawings of the Callanish sites. **National Monuments Record**, RCD/13/13—16.
Sinclair, J.	1891	**Scenes and Stories of the North of Scotland.** Edinburgh.
Somerville, B.	1912	Prehistoric Monuments in the Outer Hebrides and their Astronomical Significance. **J.R. Anthrop. Inst.**, 42, 15—52.
Stuart, J	1866	**The Sculptured Stones of Scotland** Vol. 2. Edinburgh.
Stukeley, W.	c.1720	**Commonplace Book**, ms held by **Wiltshire Archaeological and Natural History Society**, Devizes (No ms number).
Swire, O.	1966	**The Outer Hebrides and Their Legends.** London.
Thom, A.	1967	**Megalithic Sites in Britain.** Oxford.
Thom, A.	1971	**Megalithic Lunar Observatories.** Oxford.
Thom A. and Thom, A.S.	1978	**Megalithic Remains in Britain and Brittany.** Oxford.
Toland, J.	1726	**The History of the Druids.** (New edn., London, 1814.)
University of Glasgow, Department of Geography.	1978	**A Map of the Standing Stones and Circles at Callanish, Isle of Lewis, with a detailed plan of each site.** Glasgow.
Wise, T.A.	1877	Remarks on Celtic Monuments, **J. Brit. Arch. Ass.**, 33 158—169.
Wood, L.	1981	**Reflections of Airgid.** Privately circulated leaflet.
Worsaae, J.J.A.	1846	**Manuscript field notebooks** (unnumbered). **Nationalmuseet**. Copenhagen.

Recommended books on British megalithic sites generally

Burl, A.	1976	**Stone Circles of the British Isles.** London.
Hadingham, E.	1975	**Circles and Standing Stones.** London.
Heggie, H.	1981	**Megalithic Science.** London.
Mackie, E.	1977	**Science and Society in Prehistoric Britain.** London.
Michell, J	1982	**Megalithomania.** London.
Wood, J.E.	1980	**Sun Moon and Standing Stones.** Oxford

Five novels, in which Callanish plays a significant part, set partly or wholly in Lewis

Black, W.	1873	**A Princess of Thule.** London.
Gordon, S.	1975	**Suaine and the Crow God.** London
Horwood, W.	1984	**Callanish.** London.
Knight, A.	1982	**Colla's Children.** London.
Ogilvie, E.	1981	**The Silent Ones.** New York.

G. and M. Ponting Publications

Privately published books and leaflets

1977	The Standing Stones of Callanish.
1980	A mini-guide to Dun Carloway Broch.
1981	The Story of Kesgrave: Stability and Growth in a Suffolk Parish.
1981	Clach an Tursa, Carloway.
1981	Achmore Stone Circle.
1982	A mini-guide to Eoropie Teampull.
1983	A mini-guide to Shawbost Stone Circle.
1984	A mini-guide to Achmore Stone Circle.
1984	The Stones around Callanish.
1984	New Light on the Stones of Callanish.
In prep.	Callanish — Stonehenge of the Hebrides.

Unpublished reports
available for consultation at:
Stornoway Reference Library
National Museum of Antiquities of Scotland
National Monuments Record, Edinburgh.

1979	Callanish — the Documentary Record.
1981	Callanish — the Documentary Record, Part 2 — the Minor Sites.

Articles and Papers

1980 "Researches at Callanish", in **Popular Archaeology**, Oct. 1980.
1981 "Decoding the Callanish Complex — some initial results", in **Astronomy and Society in Britain during the period 4000-1500 B.C.**, ed. C.L.N. Ruggles and A.W.R. Whittle. Oxford: B.A.R.
1982 "Decoding the Callanish Complex — a progress report", in **Archaeoastronomy in the Old World**, ed. D. Heggie. Cambridge: C.U.P.
1983 "Archaeology in the Isle of Lewis" in **Scottish Archaeological Gazette**, 4, 6—10.
Jan. 1983 onwards. Regular articles on Western Isles archaeology in the **Stornoway Gazette**.
1984 "Dalmore" in **Current Archaeology**, 91, 230—235.

ACKNOWLEDGEMENTS

The research on which we have based this book began in 1975 and is still continuing. To mention by name all those individuals and organisations who have been associated with it in some way or another, on one occasion or for many years, would be quite impossible. Thus, we must apologise to those who are omitted.

Special thanks go to the inhabitants of Callanish, Garynahine and Breasclete who have shared their deep knowledge of the area. Without this local information, our research would have been a much more academic affair, rather than something which grew out of our life in the present-day Callanish community.

Comhairle nan Eilean, the Western Isles Islands Council, has been able to support us in a number of ways. We have always found their officials to be interested in our work and willing to give any assistance which they can.

The Western Isles Public Library has been very helpful over our numerous requests. We have also carried out a great deal of library research by post or on visits to Edinburgh. J.N.G. Ritchie of the RCAHMS has made available a great deal of unpublished material in the National Monuments Record. Other material has come from the National Library of Scotland, the British Library, the Public Record Office in Kew, the Nationalmuseet of Copenhagen, and the Salisbury and South Wiltshire Museum.

Patrick Ashmore, Ancient Monuments Inspector with the Scottish Development Department, has official responsibility for Callanish and directed the two seasons of excavation. We have benefited, throughout our studies, from his full co-operation and from frequent discussions in person, by post and by telephone. The chapters "The Building of Callanish" and "Callanish in the Context of Prehistoric Scotland" are based, with his permission, on a lecture which he gave in October 1983. (Thanks also to the Stornoway Gazette, where these chapters first appeared as articles.)

Trevor Cowie, formerly of the Central Excavation Unit and now of the National Museum of Antiquities, has been another constant link with the world of professional Scottish archaeology. His work at Callanish, with Sjoerd Boencke's pollen analysis, forms the foundation for the chapter "The Prehistoric Environment".

Professor Alexander Thom and Dr. A.S. Thom have constantly supported our astronomical studies and given us a great deal of advice in this area. G.R. Curtis worked closely with us and taught us, among many other things, surveying techniques. Dr. Clive Ruggles has also shown interest in our work in astronomy. We benefited a great deal from two important conferences on archaeo-astronomy and are grateful to Gordon Moir, Michael Hoskin and Douglas Heggie for making it possible for us to attend these.

Aubrey Burl, the author of many books on stone circles, has been another regular and very helpful correspondent. His ideas appear at a number of points in this book, as they must in any book on the subject today.

David Tait, the director of the 1974 "Callanish Expedition" from the Geography Department of Glasgow University, has regularly supplied information on request. Though the "Glasgow plan" of Callanish may not seem to figure prominently in this work, it is also true that new research would have been more difficult without the survey which his team undertook.

We thank too those providing illustrations, individually acknowledged in captions.

Our thanks are also due to many chance acquaintances — people we happened to meet at the site or who called at the house. Their diverse skills and interests sparked off fascinating discussions and new friendships. Our motto became "There is no such thing as a normal week"!

Last, but by no means least, our thanks to Benjamin and Rebecca, who have grown up in a mosaic of archaeological studies and helped in so many ways.

ABOUT THE AUTHORS

From 1963 till 1974, Gerald and Margaret Ponting lived at Kesgrave, near Ipswich in Suffolk. They researched, wrote and published a history of their parish. In 1974, disillusioned by the urbanisation of the English countryside, they "emigrated" to the Isle of Lewis with their young family.

By chance, their new home was in the village of Callanish. They were soon fascinated by the Standing Stones, and amazed to find that there was little readily available information about the site.

Stimulated by Alexander Thom's "Megalithic Sites in Britain", Margaret began her own research and Gerald soon joined in. They found a number of "new" sites in the area — and made important discoveries about the "main site".

In 1977, they gathered together the information that was available and wrote "The Standing Stones of Callanish". Over the next seven tourist seasons, thirteen thousand copies of this book were sold and it is frequently listed in the bibliographies of books on British megaliths.

In 1978, they entered the BBC "Chronicle" contest, and won one of the British Archaeological Awards for that year, presented by H.R.H. The Prince of Wales.

Gerald and Margaret were among the seventy invited delegates to the first International Symposium on archaeo-astronomy (the study of the relationship of ancient sites to the movements of the sun and moon), which was held at Oxford University in 1981.

The work at Callanish expanded to an interest in the island's general archaeology. On a number of occasions, excavation or survey work begun by them resulted in the arrival of a professional team from Edinburgh. Achmore Stone Circle, the fourteenth largest in Scotland, was first recorded and described as a result of their work. Margaret's long-term excavations at Dalmore Beach eventually exposed prehistoric structures and houses and resulted in a large and important collection of tools and pottery fragments. Gerald writes a regular archaeology column for the "Stornoway Gazette".

Margaret still lives at Callanish and devotes much of her time to continuing archaeological work. After nine-and-a-half years as a science teacher at the Nicolson Institute, Stornoway, Gerald returned to his native Hampshire in 1984 to expand his writing and lecturing activities.

Their various publications are listed in the bibliography.

H.R.H. The Prince of Wales with the authors.
Photograph by courtesy of The British Museum.